AF571911

Printed in the United States of America
International Standard Book Numbers
Hardcover: 0-8372-1035-6
Softcover: 0-8372-1810-1
Library of Congress Catalog Card Number 74-3881
Adapted from MEDIAMIND

in mediamind

MEDIA
HOW MANY MEDIA DO YOU KNOW?

MIND
WHICH MEDIUM DO YOU KNOW BEST?

HAVE ANOTHER SANDWICH?
THIS COFFEE IS TERRIFIC!
READY ON CAMERA TWO?
I-D-E-A HEY! THERE'S AN IDEA IN MEDIA
DIRECTOR
I'LL HAVE THE SCRIPT CHANGE READY IN A MINUTE
WHAT'S MEDIA, ANYWAY?
SHOULD THAT BE MEDIUM?

I USE MANY MEDIA IN MY WORK
I'M SORRY OPERATOR, THE DIRECTOR'S BUSY RIGHT NOW. WOULD YOU LIKE TO LEAVE A MESSAGE?
WE'VE GOT MEDIA — BRING ON THE MIND
CABLE FOR MR. DIRECTOR
AM I TOO LATE FOR THE AUDITIONS? I'M A MEDIUM
SO AM I
I'M A MEDIUM
YOU'RE KIDDING — I AM
UPON THE SWANE-E RIVER,

MEMORIES
titudes
THEORIES
information
INTUITION
HUNCHES
DO YOU WANT MIND BEHIND MEDIA?
THEY SHOULD BE SIDE BY SIDE
BELIEFS
FACTS
pretations
WHAT ABOUT PUTTING MIND OVER MEDIA?

Perceptions
feelings
CALCULATIONS
JUDGEMENT
imagination
PRESS
I'M COVERING THIS PRODUCTION FOR MY MAGAZINE - CAN I HAVE AN INTERVIEW?
MIND's COMING THROUGH, NOW
DREAMS
Curiosity
MESSAGES
MAYBE I'LL FIND A NEWSPAPER STORY ON THIS SET

MEDIA . . . MIND . . .
What's the connection?
MEDIAMIND
OUTPUT 1
OUTPUT 2
MEDIA
MIND
FINAL OUTPUT

media magazine

Vol. 1, No. 2

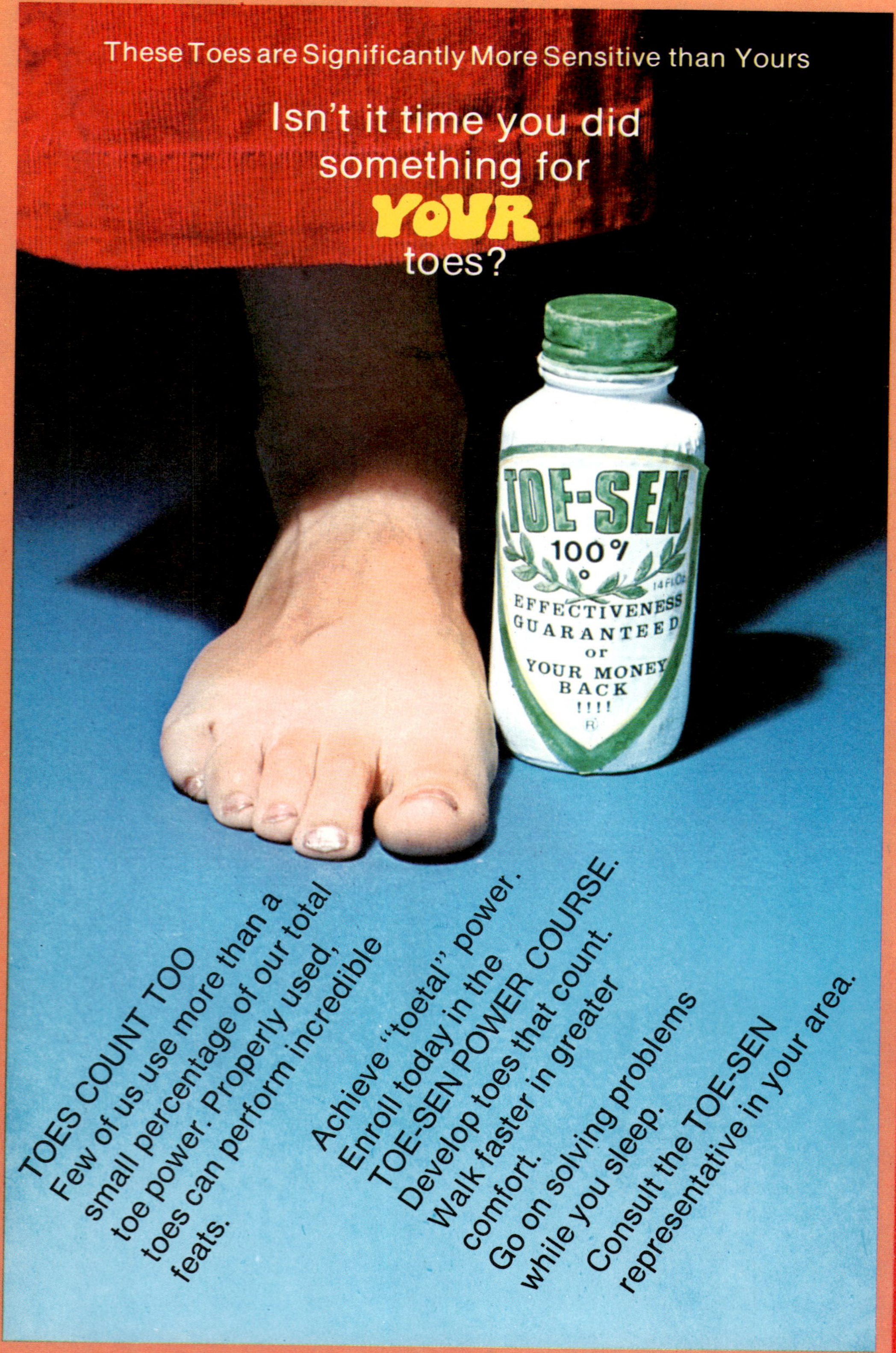

These Toes are Significantly More Sensitive than Yours

Isn't it time you did something for YOUR toes?

TOE-SEN
100%
EFFECTIVENESS GUARANTEED OR YOUR MONEY BACK !!!!

TOES COUNT TOO
Few of us use more than a small percentage of our total toe power. Properly used, toes can perform incredible feats.

Achieve "toetal" power.
Enroll today in the TOE-SEN POWER COURSE.
Develop toes that count.
Walk faster in greater comfort.
Go on solving problems while you sleep.
Consult the TOE-SEN representative in your area.

SENSE-A-TOE MAGAZINE helped me.

Why don't you liberate your toes today?

Send no money—10 day trial.
Please send me a free copy of SENSE-A-TOE MAGAZINE. If not delighted within 10 days I may return the magazine and owe nothing.

Name: ________________

Address: ________________

DO YOU HAVE SOMETHING TO SELL?
—A PRODUCT THAT WILL IMPROVE THE MESSAGE SENT AND RECEIVED BY EYES? EARS? NOSE?
Imagine the impact of your advertisements in *MEdia Magazine!*

experiments from media magazine's research department

Watch a TV program with the sound turned off. Make notes of what you think is happening. Compare your version with that of a friend who watched the same program.

Stand near the fruit and vegetable section in the supermarket. Close your eyes for a minute. How many messages reach you?

Use plasticine or clay to spell out a message. Blindfold a friend and watch how your message is interpreted. Try tracing a message in sand. Can your friend interpret it?

Try to locate areas on your tongue that register SWEET, SOUR, SALTY, and BITTER tastes. You will need:

sugar dissolved in a little water
lemon juice
salt dissolved in a little water
instant coffee dissolved in a little water

Test the tip, the sides, the middle, and the back of your tongue by dipping a toothpick into one mixture then touching each area in turn. When you have done this with the four mixtures, you are ready to make a map of your tongue.

On your map, mark where you taste:

ice cream
cough syrup
cheese
honey
tomatoes

Do bodies talk?

This interesting question is posed by Snap Gordon, *MEDIA MAGAZINE'S* roving photographer.

TA

PRESENT

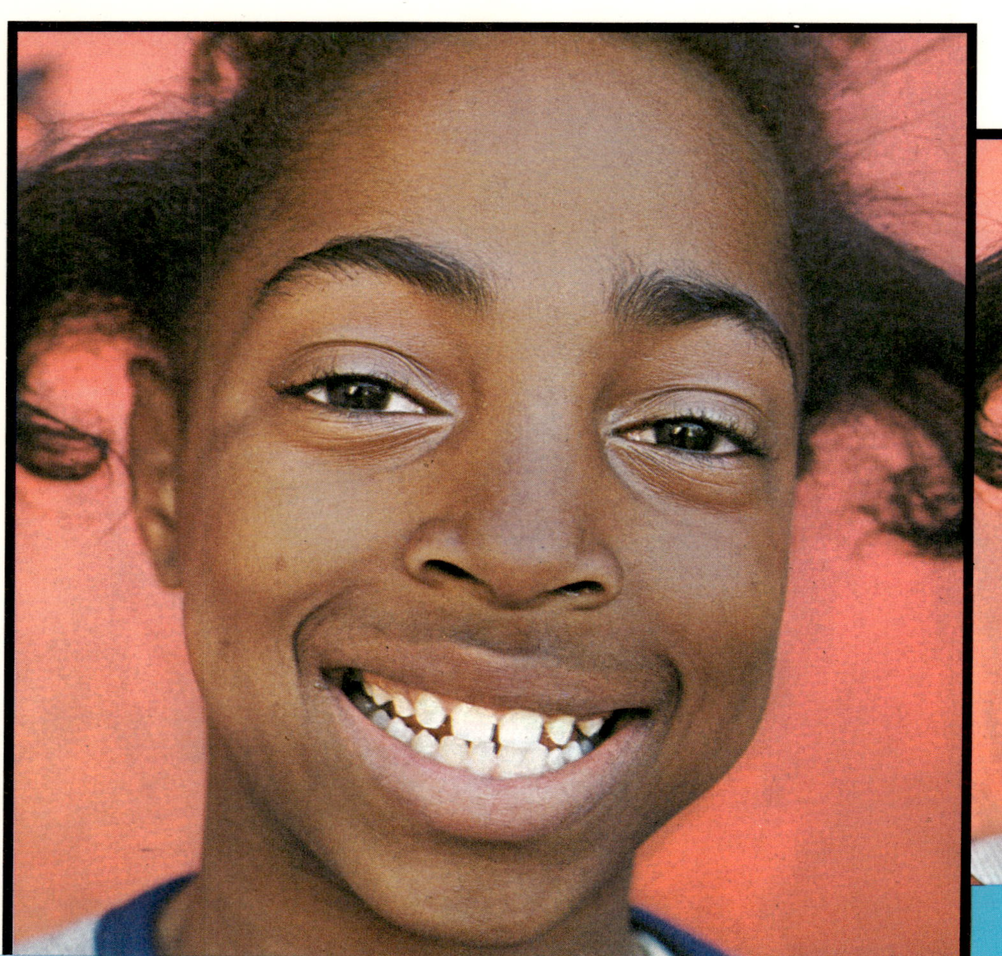

NODS AND NUDGES AN ILLUSTRATED DICTIONARY OF BODYTALK

by R. E. Seeven
Reviewed by Senta Kabel

This is the most unusual dictionary ever printed. It consists largely of photographs. When I asked author R. E. Seeven why he had produced a photographic dictionary, he replied, with a shrug, "Words are not enough to describe bodytalk." In his book, Mr. Seeven has skillfully used the stop-action camera to show in precise detail how bodies talk. Mr. Seeven treats such interesting gestures and expressions as frowns, grins, grimaces, nods, nudges, prods, scowls, smirks, sneers, waves, smiles and winks.

Here is his entry for SMILE: Smile: a facial expression formed by an upward curving of the corners of the mouth, sometimes revealing the teeth. A smile may indicate pleasure, amusement, affection, disbelief, or scorn.

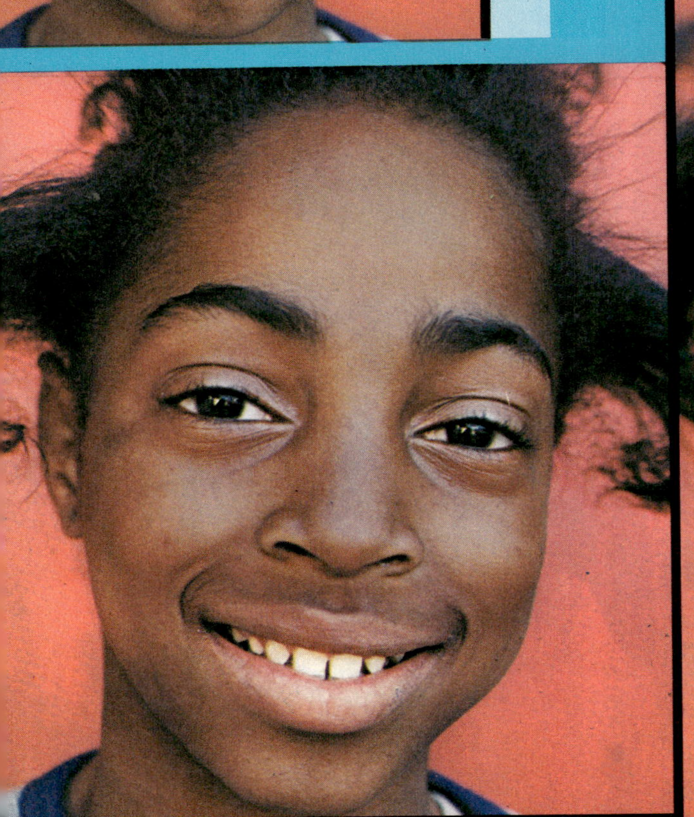

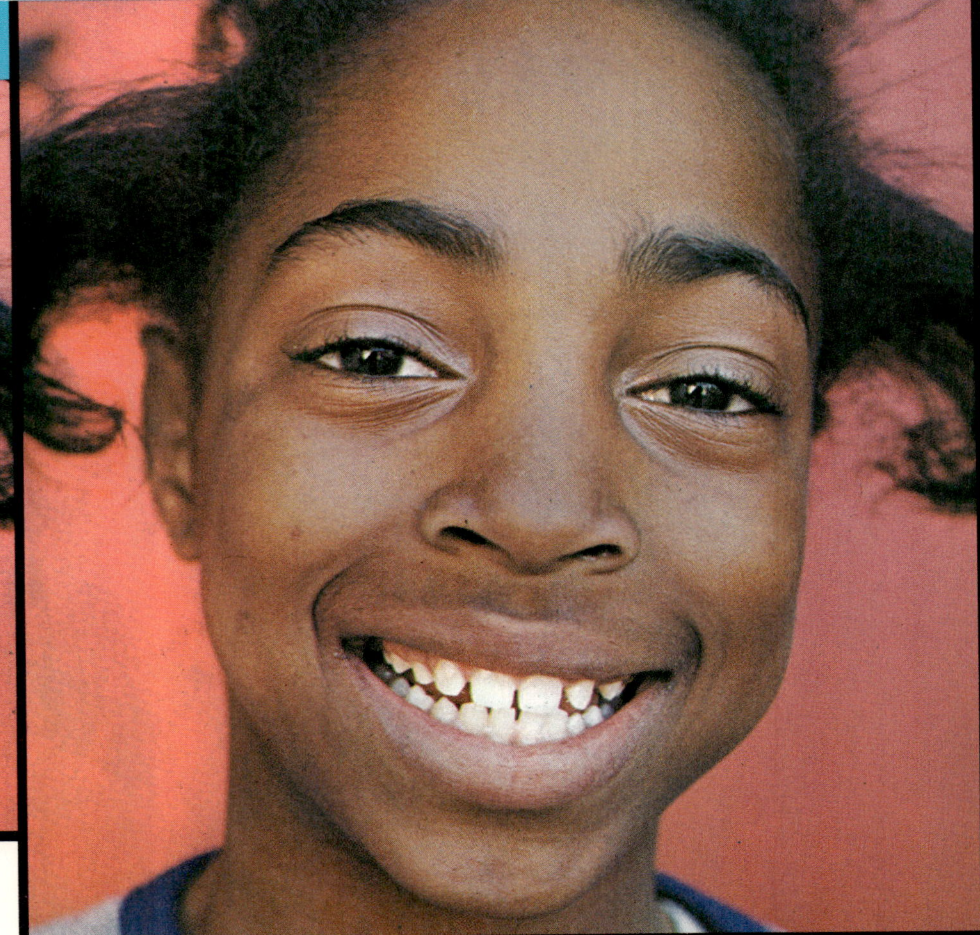

Professor Biodelve

A CONVERSATION WITH PROFESSOR BIODELVE

MEdia Magazine presents a scoop interview with the famous Professor Biodelve, author of *Monkey's Tails, Lizards, Lions and Lapdogs, From Tadpole to Frog in Several Leaps,* and *The Earthworm Underground, a study in depth.* The professor at present is studying a creature he calls Mediamite. Our reporter interviewed the professor in his remote hideaway laboratory. It is with pride that we present this exclusive interview.

Int. What are you working on at present, Professor?
P.B. An interesting little creature I've just come across in my research. I keep it in that cage over there.
Int. But the cage is empty.
P.B. Hmm—oh well—my assistant must have taken Mediamite to be photographed.
Int. Mediamite?
P.B. That's what I've called it... tiny message-receiver and message-sender. Of course it has other functions, but I'm not interested in them.
Int. Quite so. Could you tell me how Mediamite receives messages?
P.B. Gladly. It has two sound-wave receptors. Queer little things—they look like tiny cabbage leaves—all crinkly.
Int. What an interesting description!
P.B. These receptors seem to operate twenty-four hours a day.
Int. Non-stop, eh? What sorts of sounds does Mediamite receive?
P.B. Soft ones, loud ones, low ones, high ones. A great range. In fact, tests I have conducted show that Mediamite can hear sounds so soft or high-pitched only my dog can pick them up.
Int. Goodness me! Has Mediamite any other way of receiving messages?
P.B. Yes, indeed. Two light-wave

receptors. These operate in both dim and bright light. In dim light a mechanism opens the receptor to ensure maximum intake of light waves. Like a camera lens opening.
Int. Do the light wave receptors also operate twenty-four hours a day?
P.B. No. Only for a few hours at most. Then a shutter covers each receptor.
Int. Like a lens cap on a camera?
P.B. Yes, yes! Just like that. You catch on quick. Ever thought of taking up science?
Int. Er... no, Professor. Has Mediamite any other way to receive messages?
P.B. Glad you asked that. I've discovered that the surface of Mediamite is covered in invisible sensors that register the slightest contact with external objects, especially sharp ones—like a pin.
Int. What a rare creature! What happens to all the messages Mediamite receives?
P.B. Another good question! And I'm not sure of the answer. It's my hunch that Mediamite has some sort of message-bank—where incoming messages are deposited. But where the bank is, and how long the messages stay there—I've no idea.
Int. I think you have at last found your life's work, Professor. Could you tell me something about Mediamite's transmitter system?
P.B. Ah yes! A fascinating aspect of my research! Mediamite has an

unusual sound-wave sender. It emits a great variety of noises—some soft, almost birdlike—others very loud and penetrating. The distance these shrill sounds carry is quite remarkable. In recent experiments I have found that they will penetrate three layers of sandbags and a bank vault door.
Int. Amazing, Professor.
P.B. And what's more, when the Mediamite emits those shrill sounds, a red glow spreads over its surface.
Int. Perhaps it overheats.
P.B. Never thought of that! Good suggestion. I'll set up some tests to see.
Int. Do these sounds mean anything?
P.B. I think so. I'm having them monitored by a tape recorder right

around the clock. With enough data we might be able to break the code.
Int. Rather similar to the research going on with dolphins, I take it?
P.B. Yes, very like that. But more advanced, of course. I think we've

got a lot to show those dolphin boys.
Int. Does Mediamite send messages in any other way?
P.B. It has four extensions that often wave about a great deal—especially when the sound emitter is working hard. Whether these movements are a way of sending messages I don't know. But I'm working on it.
Int. Can you tell me about it?
P.B. Well... I'd rather not... top secret you know...
Int. Please, Professor Biodelve! Think of the millions of readers breathlessly waiting for news of your latest research.
P.B. Well, if you put it like that... The truth is, I'm working with a videomonitor.
Int. No!
P.B. Yes!
Int. That's brilliant. A stroke of genius! Er... what's a video thingummy?
P.B. A round-the-clock TV camera that records every movement Mediamite makes. I'll catch every wave, every twiddle, every flicker!
Int. Every flicker! Imagine!
P.B. And one day I'll decode the signals of Mediamite.
Int. Good heavens!
P.B. And I'll write another book about it.
Int. Words fail me!
P.B. In three volumes!
Int. I'm dizzy.
P.B. A best seller...
Int. Could I have a glass of water?
P.B. Translated into twenty languages!
Int. My ears are ringing!
P.B. I'll call it "Messages from Mediamite"!
Int. (Gasp!) You're a genius, Professor!

The Professor photographed in front of the empty Mediamite cage

me

BODYTALK PHOTOGRAPH DISPLAY

MEdia Magazine suggests that interested groups run their own bodytalk photograph display. Photos from newspapers and magazines, as well as those specially taken for the occasion, could be mounted on cardboard and displayed with suitable captions.

Public announcement

Why not form a Mediamite watchers association in your community? Collect information, take photographs, formulate theories. Let others know what you find out.

MEdia magazine WANTS YOU!

WANTED: Media Expert with at least ten years experience. Must be a practiced communicator, experienced in transmitting complicated messages and skilled in receiving and interpreting similar messages. Write an account of your message receiving and sending ability.

DOES THIS MEAN YOU?

next issue

MEdia Magazine features:

A brilliant short story, "It Started with a Scowl and Ended with a Wink"

A photographic essay entitled, "From Grimace to Grin"

An exciting article, "Finger Painting—is it here to stay?" illustrated with unusual paintings of and by fingers

Child Wonder: A fascinating interview with a child who has X-ray vision

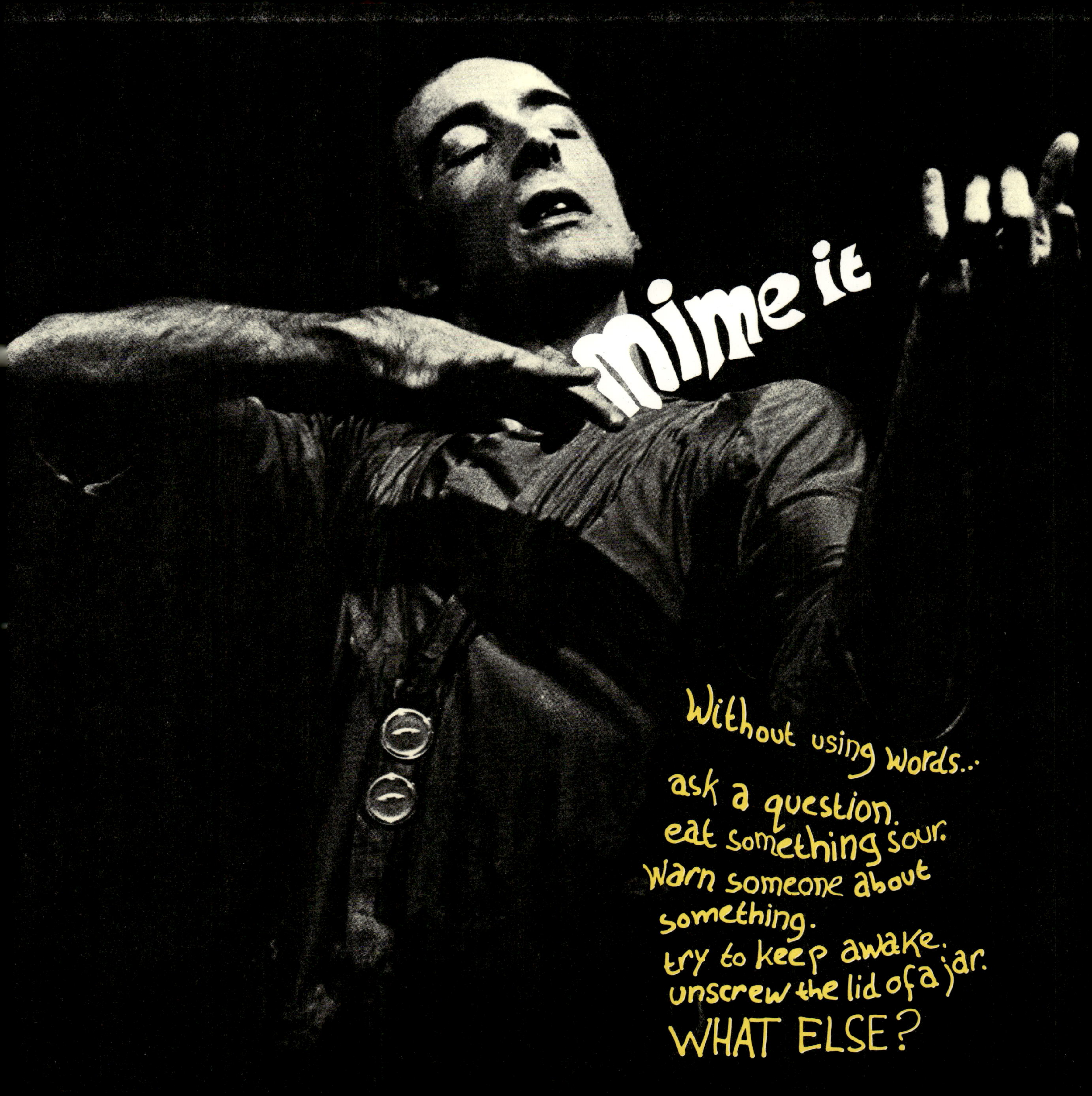

mime it

Without using words...
ask a question.
eat something sour.
warn someone about something.
try to keep awake.
unscrew the lid of a jar.
WHAT ELSE?

the box

washing an elephant

unfolding
lookout

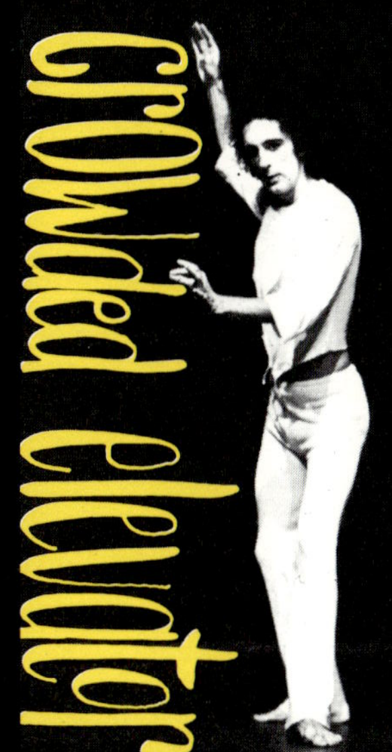
crowded elevator

on guard

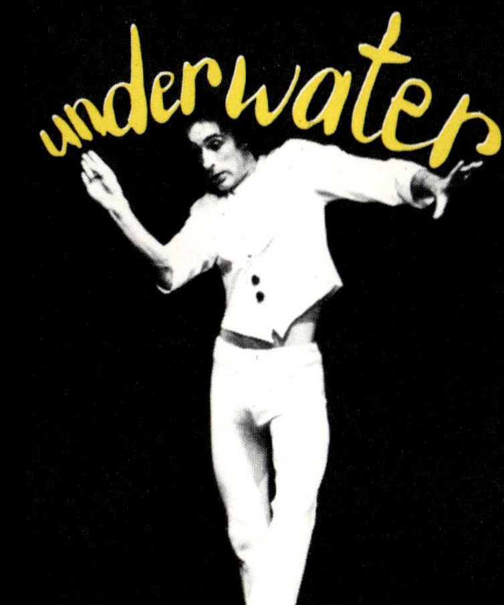
underwater

spring

free at last

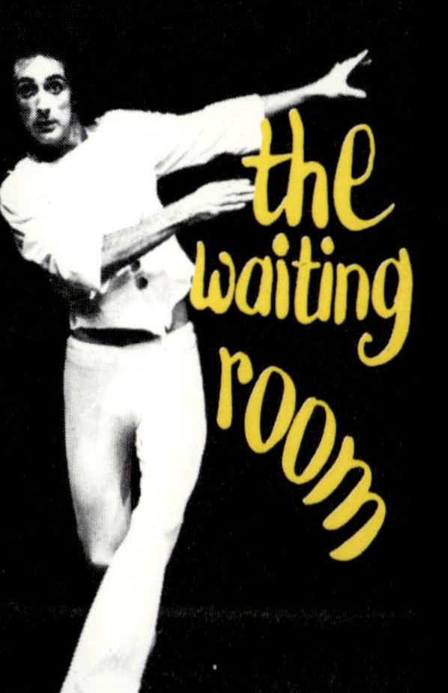
the waiting room

in space

freefall

the tunnel

a telephone conversation

a conversation with a giant

machines

an argument

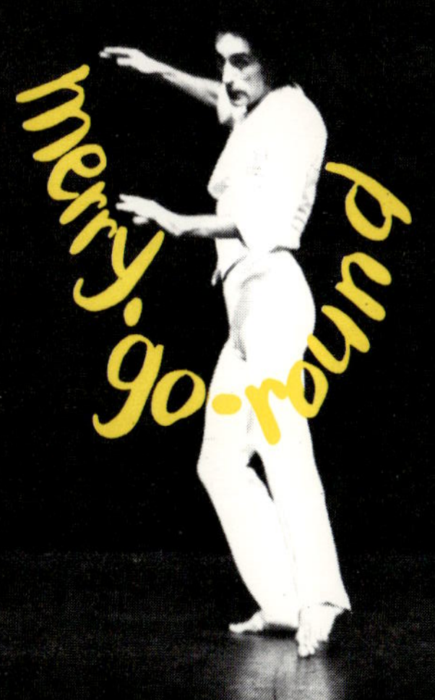
merry-go-round

dining out

ping pong

the grasshopper

the storm

try these

TRY THESE ON
PUT THEM ON
RELUCTANTLY

nervously
HURRIEDLY
HOW
ELSE?

MIRROR MIMES

Choose a friend to be your mirror image.

try combing your hair
brushing your teeth
washing your face
what else?

My silent scrapbook

Night was falling fast. Darkness blurred the edges of the treacherous trail. Storm clouds hid the helpful moon. Could the lone messenger get his message through?

"I want you to take your report cards home tonight. Have your parents sign them."

MAN'S BEST FRIEND GUARDS THE SLEEPING HOUSE.

"I must warn the village!"

"Take these orders to the General. He must hold the fort at any cost."

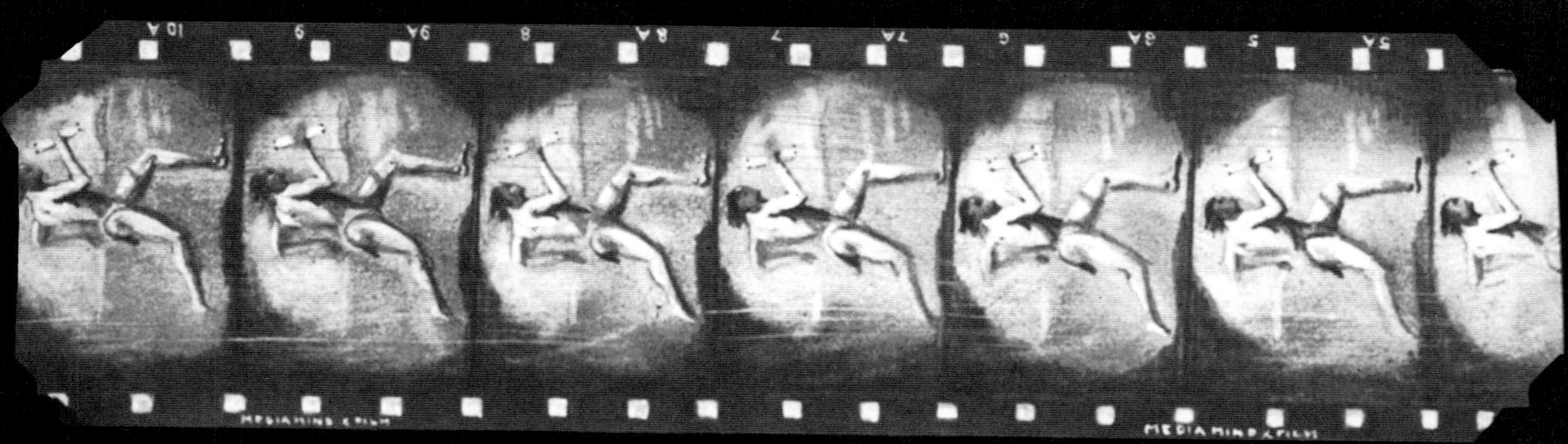

"The message must reach the rest of the tribe before sunset."

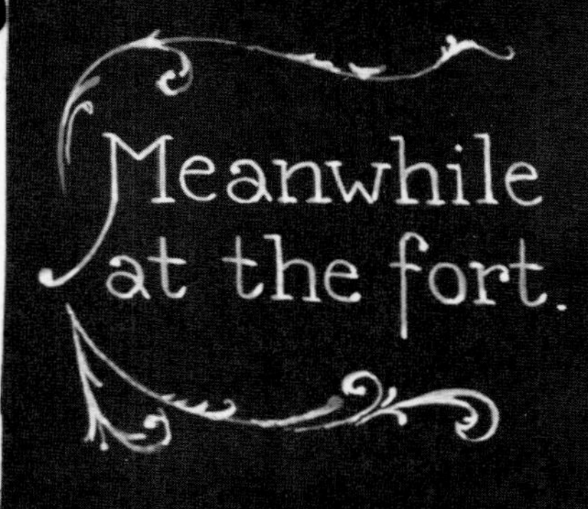

"I must get the message to the Pharaoh."

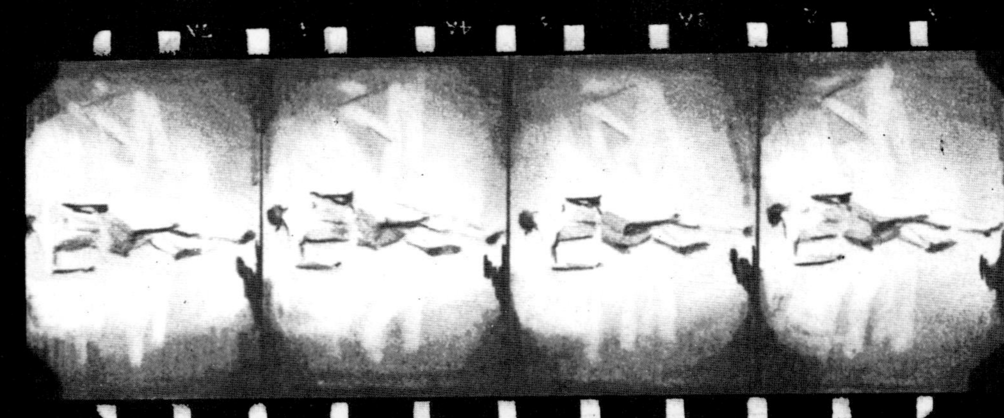

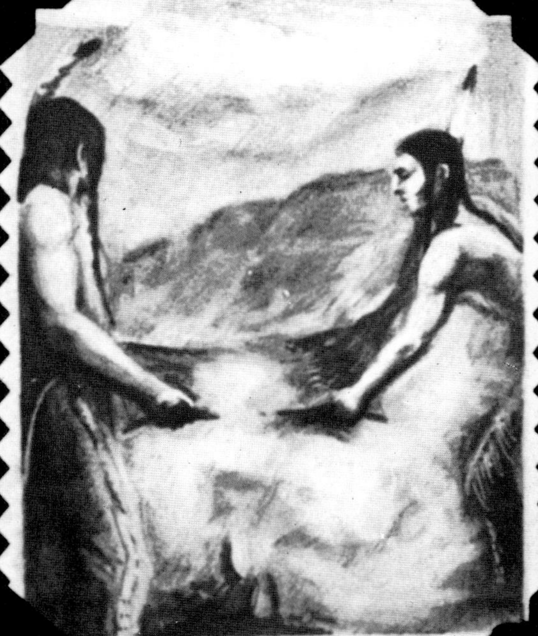

TO BE
SORTED

monkey messages

by Gerald Durrell

Weekes, the red-headed mangabey, came by his name owing to his cry. Whenever you went near his cage, he would open his mouth wide and shout "Weekes, weekes" at the top of his voice.

He was a delicate shade of gray all over, except for a band of white fur 'round his neck and the top of his head, which was a bright mahogany red. His face was a very dark gray and his eyelids were creamy white. Normally, you could not see these, but when he greeted you he would raise his eyebrows and lower his lids so suddenly, it looked as though his eyes had been covered by white shutters.

Weekes was very bored with living in a cage by himself with no one to play with, but I could not give him a mate, as he was the only one of his species that I had. He did not realize this, however, for all round him he could hear and smell other monkeys and he thought it very unfair of me not to let him leave his cage and go to play with them. He decided the best thing to do was to tunnel his way out of the side when I was not looking.

He had discovered a small gap between the boards of the side of his cage and set to work with fingers and teeth to widen it. The wood was very hard, and it was only after much picking and biting that he was able to work off a small splinter. I kept a cautious eye on the hole to make sure it did not get any larger, but Weekes did not know this and thought I knew nothing about it. He would spend hours biting and scratching at the wood, but as soon as he heard me coming he would leap up on to his perch and sit there, looking as innocent as possible, raising his eyebrows and showing his white eyelids, blinking at me cheerfully, in the hope of persuading me that he was the very last monkey in the camp to do anything wicked.

I did not do anything about Weekes's hole, for I thought that as soon as he found out how hard the wood was he would soon give it up. To my surprise, exactly the opposite happened. He became so interested that he used to spend every available moment biting and scratching and sucking at the wood. Every time I came on the scene, however, there he was sitting on his perch without a care in the world, and if it had not been for the few splinters that stuck to the hairs of his chin, I should not have known that he was still going on with his mining operations. He seemed so convinced that I did not know about his secret passage that one day I thought I would give him a surprise.

I had just given him a bowl of milk, so he was not expecting me back at his cage for at least an hour. Refreshed by his drink, he set to work on his hole. I allowed him enough time to get well started and then I crept down the line of cages. There was Weekes, squatting on the floor, with a grim, determined expression on his face, tugging with both hands at quite a large splinter of wood. It was a very tough piece, and although he pulled at it with all his might, it would not part company with the side of the cage, and so he became angrier and angrier, muttering to himself and screwing up his face in the most frightening grimaces. Just as he was bending forwards to see if he could bite through the annoying splinter, I asked him in a stern voice what he thought he was doing.

He jumped as though I had jabbed him with a pin, and then glanced over his shoulder with a horrified and guilty expression on his face. I asked him again what he thought he was up to, and, giving me a feeble grin, he made a half-hearted attempt to show me his eyelids. Seeing that I was not to be distracted, he sheepishly let go of the splinter and seizing his empty milk pot, leapt on to his perch, where he was overcome with embarrassment and put the pot over his face and fell backwards off the perch on to the bottom of the cage.

He looked so ridiculous that I had to laugh, and so he decided that I must have forgiven him. He climbed back on to his perch, wearing the pot like a tin helmet on his head, and then fell off the perch again. This time he fell on his head and hurt himself, so he had to come to the bars and have his paws held until he felt better.

Now he realized I knew all about his hole, he gave up being so secretive about it and used to work away in full view of me. If I scolded him, he would repeat his trick of putting the pot over his face and falling backwards off the perch; and if I laughed he would assume that he had been forgiven and go back to work. Just as a precaution, however, I nailed a bit of wire over the outside of his hole, which he was extremely annoyed about when he discovered it. When he found he could not shift the wire, he rather reluctantly gave up his tunneling, but never forgot his trick of falling off his perch backwards, and would always do it when he knew I was angry with him, in order to try to pacify me.

WHAT'S THE
MESSAGE?

WHAT'S THE
MESSA

GE

She Can't See! She Can't Hear!

by William Gibson

TIME: *The 1880's.*

PLACE: *In and around the Keller homestead in Tuscumbia, Alabama.*

It is night over the Keller homestead.

Inside, three adults in the bedroom are grouped around a crib, in lamplight. They have been through a long vigil, and it shows in their tired bearing and disarranged clothing. One is a young gentlewoman with a sweet girlish face, KATE KELLER; *the second is an elderly* DOCTOR, *stethoscope at neck, thermometer in fingers; the third is a hearty gentleman in his forties with chin whiskers,* CAPTAIN ARTHUR KELLER.

DOCTOR: She'll live.

KATE: Thank God.

(The DOCTOR *leaves them together over the crib, packs his bag.)*

DOCTOR: You're a pair of lucky parents. I can tell you now, I thought she wouldn't.

KELLER: Nonsense, the child's a Keller, she has the constitution of a goat. She'll outlive us all.

DOCTOR [AMIABLY]: Yes, especially if some of you Kellers don't get a night's sleep. I mean you, Mrs. Keller....

KATE: Doctor, don't be merely considerate, will my girl be all right?

DOCTOR: Oh, by morning she'll be knocking down Captain Keller's fences again.

KATE: And isn't there anything we should do?

KELLER [JOVIAL]: Put up stronger fencing, ha?

DOCTOR: Just let her get well, she knows how to do it better than we do.

(He is packed, ready to leave.)

Main thing is the fever's gone, these things come and go in infants, never know why. Call it acute congestion of the stomach and brain.

KELLER: I'll see you to your buggy, Doctor.

DOCTOR: I've never seen a baby, more vitality, that's the truth.

(He beams a good night at the baby and KATE, *and* KELLER *leads him downstairs with a lamp. They go down the porch steps, and across the yard, where the* DOCTOR *goes off left;* KELLER *stands with the lamp aloft.* KATE *meanwhile is bent lovingly over the crib, which emits a bleat; her finger is playful with the baby's face.)*

KATE: Hush. Don't you cry now, you've been trouble enough. Call it acute congestion, indeed, I don't see what's so cute about a congestion, just because it's yours. We'll have your father run an editorial in his paper, the wonders of modern medicine, they don't know what they're curing even when they cure it....

(But she breaks off, puzzled, moves her finger before the baby's eyes.)

Will have to—Helen?

(Now she moves her hand, quickly.)

Helen.

(She snaps her fingers at the baby's eyes twice, and her hand falters; after a moment she calls out, loudly.)

Captain. Captain, will you come—

(But she stares at the baby, and her next call is directly at her ears.)

Captain!

(And now, still staring, KATE *screams.* KELLER *in the yard hears it, and runs with the lamp back to the house.* KATE *screams again, her look intent on the baby and terrible.* KELLER *hurries in and up.)*

KELLER: Katie? What's wrong?

KATE: Look.

(She makes a pass with her hand in the crib, at the baby's eyes.)

KELLER: What, Katie? She's well, she needs only time to—

KATE: She can't see. Look at her eyes.

(She takes the lamp from him, moves it before the child's face.)

She can't *see!*

KELLER [HOARSELY]: Helen.

KATE: Or hear. When I screamed she didn't blink. Not an eyelash—

KELLER: Helen. Helen!

KATE: She can't *hear* you!

KELLER: *Helen!*

When words began...

by Helen Keller

The most important day I remember in all my life is the one on which my teacher, Anne Mansfield Sullivan, came to me. I am filled with wonder when I consider the immeasurable contrasts between the two lives which it connects. It was the third of March, 1887, three months before I was seven years old.

The morning after my teacher came she led me into her room and gave me a doll. The little blind children at the Perkins Institution had sent it and Laura Bridgman had dressed it; but I did not know this until afterward. When I had played with it a little while, Miss Sullivan slowly spelled into my hand the word "d-o-l-l." I was at once interested in this finger play and tried to imitate it. When I finally succeeded in making the letters correctly I was flushed with childish pleasure and pride. Running downstairs to my mother I held up my hand and made the letters for doll. I did not know that I was spelling a word or even that words existed; I was simply making my fingers go in monkey-like imitation. In the days that followed I learned to spell in this uncomprehending way a great many words, among them *pin, hat, cup* and a few verbs like *sit, stand* and *walk.* But my teacher had been with me several weeks before I understood that everything has a name.

One day, while I was playing with my new doll, Miss Sullivan put my big rag doll into my lap also, spelled "d-o-l-l" and tried to make me understand that "d-o-l-l" applied to both. Earlier in the day we had had a tussle over the words "m-u-g" and "w-a-t-e-r." Miss Sullivan had tried to impress it upon me that "m-u-g" is *mug* and that "w-a-t-e-r" is *water,* but I persisted in confounding the two. In despair she had dropped the subject for the time, only to renew it at the first opportunity. I became impatient at her repeated attempts and, seizing the new doll, I dashed it upon the floor. I was keenly delighted when I felt the fragments of the broken doll at my feet. Neither sorrow nor regret followed my passionate outburst. I had not loved the doll. In the still, dark world in which I lived there was no strong sentiment of tenderness. I felt my teacher sweep the fragments to one side of the hearth, and I had a sense of satisfaction that the cause of my discomfort was removed. She brought me my hat, and I knew I was going out into the warm sunshine. This thought, if a wordless sensation may be called a thought, made me hop and skip with pleasure.

We walked down the path to the well-house, attracted by the fragrance of the honeysuckle with which it was covered. Some one was drawing water and my teacher placed my hand under the spout. As the cool stream gushed over one hand she spelled into the other the word *water,* first slowly, then rapidly. I stood still, my whole attention fixed upon the motions of her fingers. Suddenly I felt a misty consciousness as of something forgotten—a thrill of returning thought; and somehow the mystery of language was revealed to me. I knew then that "w-a-t-e-r" meant the wonderful cool something that was flowing over my hand. That living word awakened my soul, gave it light, hope, joy, set it free! There were barriers still, it is true, but barriers that could in time be swept away.

I left the well-house eager to learn. Everything had a name, and each name gave birth to a new thought. As we returned to the house every object which I touched seemed to quiver with life. That was because I saw everything with the strange, new sight that had come to me. On entering the door I remembered the doll I had broken. I felt my way to the hearth and picked up the pieces. I tried vainly to put them together. Then my eyes filled with tears; for I realized what I had done, and for the first time I felt repentance and sorrow.

WOW!
take a letter Miss Smith
MEETCHA ROUND THE CORNER
would you like it delivered?
MY FEET ARE KILLING ME
THE MEETING WILL PLEASE COME TO ORDER
Mutter!
QUANTO COSTA?
This coffee's cold
COMMENT AL
If you stop crying i'll buy you an ice cream
haven't seen you
PRIME RIB ROAST
RED OR BLUE BRAND

have the exact fare ready please
SCRAM!
sunnyside up
Il conto per favore
i'm sorry Mr Smith is in conference
HOE GAAT HET MET U?
what number are you calling?
low pressure area
centered
ONE-TWO-THREE, O'LEARY
SEE YOU TOMORROW
AUF WIEDERSEHEN
fill 'er up
someone should sort out all this talk
linguists do
so can we!

JUNIOR LINGUIST
JUNIOR LINGUIST
JUNIOR LINGUIST
JUNIOR LINGUIST
JUNIOR LINGUIST
STOP
TELEPHONE

Thibault
100'
NORTH YORK
McALPINE

SOME PEOPLE SAY "GUNNA", OTHERS SAY "GOING TO". WHAT DO YOU SAY?
DEPENDS ON WHO I'M SAYING IT TO
MY GRANDPA SAYS "AIN'T"
I WENT TO AN AUCTION. YOU SHOULD HAVE HEARD THE AUCTIONEER!
DID YOU GET ANY "SIRS" OR "MADAMS" AT THE STORE? I CAUGHT SOME ON MY TAPE-LISTEN
THERE'S A GREEK FAMILY ON OUR STREET-THEY LET ME RECORD A CONVERSATION AT DINNERTIME
JUNIOR LINGUIST
JUNIOR LINGUIST MEETING
AGENDA
GROUP 1 Young Talk
-baby babble
-kindergarten report
GROUP 2 Formal Talk
-in school
-to official people
-special ceremonies
GROUP 3 Playground Talk
GROUP 4 Sport Talk
-player talk
-fan talk
-coach, umpire talk
-commentator talk
GROUP 5 Newcomer's Talk
GROUP 6 Special Talk
-auctioneers, dentists,
-doctors, plumbers,
-mechanics, musicians.
GROUP 7 Store Talk
-customer talk
-manager talk
-demonstrator talk

HOW CAN WE PRESENT OUR REPORT?
LET'S PUT SOME OF IT INTO A PLAY
WE'LL NEED SOME CHARTS
COULDN'T WE JUST PLAY THE TAPES AND GET EVERYONE TO LISTEN?
MA MA MA
WE NEED ONE MORE VISIT TO THE KINDERGARTEN
I TAPED MY BABY SISTER'S FIRST WORD. SHE'S BEEN SAYING IT FOR WEEKS
I WANT TO HEAR IF BILLY STILL SAYS "I FEEDED THE RABBIT"
IF YOU WANT TO SEE HOW LANGUAGE WORKS HAVE A LOOK AT MY STORY SPINNER

STORY SPINNER

What stories do you get?

an you spare 75¢
a cup of coffee?"
"Darling - where did you get that hat?"
"let's be friends"
"Whew - I've worked hard today"
TAXI
FACE TO FACE
NEON LIGHTS

MESSAGES
MESSAGE
Message
MESSAGE
MESSAGES
messages
MESSAGE
messages
Messages

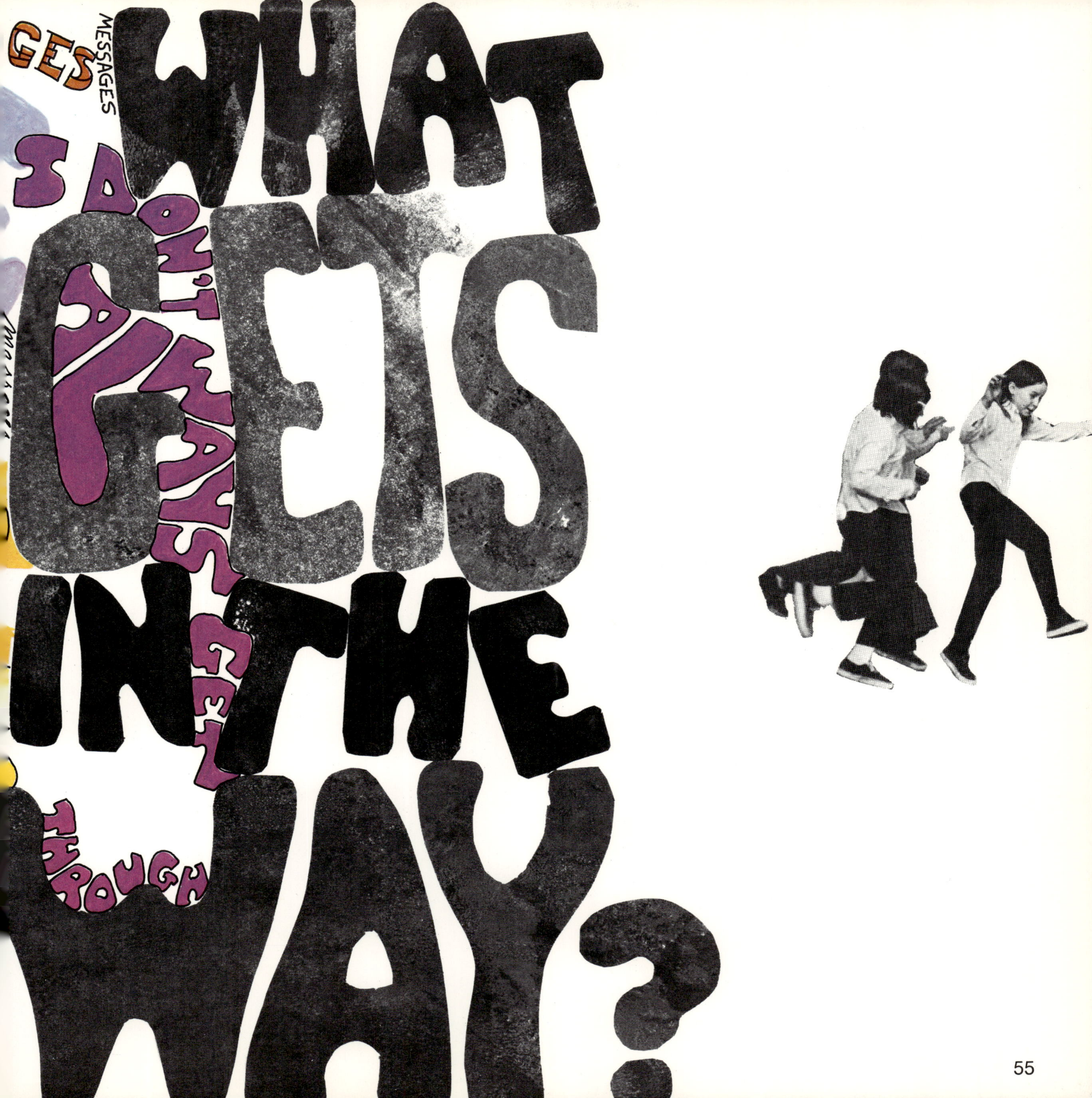
WHAT GETS IN THE WAY?
MESSAGES
GES
I DON'T ALWAYS GET THROUGH

HAVE YOU HEARD?
BILLY'S NOT HOME - HE'S GONE TO THE HOSPITAL TO SEE HIS AUNT MARY
WHERE'S BILLY?
HE'S GONE TO THE HOSPITAL
HE SAID I COULD BORROW HIS BIKE
NO YOU CAN'T - IT'S BROKEN
DID YOU HEAR THAT BILLY HAD A TERRIBLE ACCIDENT ON HIS BIKE! HE HAD TO GO TO THE HOSPITAL
OOH - I SAW AN AMBULANCE ABOUT TEN O'CLOCK THIS MORNING

I THOUGHT I HEARD A SIREN WHEN I WAS SHOPPING
BILLY'S HAD A SERIOUS ACCIDENT. THEY HAD TO RUSH HIM TO THE HOSPITAL BY AMBULANCE AT TEN O'CLOCK THIS MORNING
I WANT YOU TO TAKE THESE TO BILLY IN THE HOSPITAL. THE POOR BOY IS CRITICALLY ILL
I'M TAKING THESE TO BILLY - HE'S IN THE HOSPITAL
YOU'VE HEARD ALREADY. NEWS TRAVELS FAST AROUND HERE
BILLY'S ALLERGIC TO FLOWERS
THEY'LL HAVE TO CALL IN A SPECIALIST
THEY CAN'T OPERATE ON BILLY BECAUSE OF ALL HIS ALLERGIES
MY FATHER WAS TREATED FOR HIS ALLERGIES BY A SPECIALIST FROM AMSTERDAM
IT TAKES A LOT OF MONEY TO FLY A SPECIALIST FROM AMSTERDAM
LET'S HAVE A MILES FOR BILLY MARCH TO RAISE ENOUGH MONEY TO FLY IN A SPECIALIST TO PERFORM THE OPERATION

MILES FOR BILLY
WHO'S BILLY ANYWAY?
HE'S THE KID WHO HAD THE TERRIBLE ACCIDENT ON HIS BIKE
I HEARD BILLY WAS TRAINING FOR A BIKE RACE IN EUROPE
TOO BAD ABOUT THE ACCIDENT - IT WILL AFFECT HIS CHANCES FOR THE RACE
YOU'D THINK HIS PARENTS WOULD HAVE ENOUGH MONEY TO SEND HIM TO EUROPE. HIS FATHER'S A SPECIALIST
HEY AUNT MARY - LOOK AT THE CROWD! I WONDER WHAT THE MARCH IS ALL ABOUT?
AND ISN'T HIS AUNT A WEALTHY WOMAN?
MARY'S BIKE HOSPITAL
IT'LL PROBABLY BE ON THE NEWS TONIGHT. HAND ME THAT SPROCKET, BILLY, AND WE'LL HAVE THIS BIKE OF YOURS FIXED IN A MINUTE.
MARY

something
overheard
Tell about the time you overheard
something you
weren't meant to hear.
How did you feel?
What did you do?

And Then
FIBBING FIBBING FIBBING FIBBING
BRAGGING BRAGGING BRAGGING
BOASTING BOASTING BOASTING

There are Lies
WHITE LIES
Make Believe
Does everyone tell lies?
Is it ever all right to tell a lie?

RIDDLES IN THE DARK

by J.R.R. Tolkein

Deep down here by the dark water lived old Gollum, a small slimy creature. I don't know where he came from, nor who or what he was. He was Gollum—as dark as darkness, except for two big round pale eyes in his thin face. He had a little boat, and he rowed about quite quietly on the lake; for lake it was, wide and deep and deadly cold. He paddled it with large feet dangling over the side, but never a ripple did he make. Not he. He was looking out of his pale limp-like eyes for blind fish, which he grabbed with his long fingers as quick as thinking. He liked meat too.

Goblin he thought good, when he could get it; but he took care they never found him out. He just throttled them from behind, if they ever came down alone anywhere near the edge of the water, while he was prowling about. . . .

Actually Gollum lived on a slimy island of rock in the middle of the lake. He was watching Bilbo now from the distance with his pale eyes like telescopes. Bilbo could not see him, but he was wondering a lot about Bilbo, for he could see that he was no goblin at all.

Gollum got into his boat and shot off from the island, while Bilbo was sitting on the brink altogether flummoxed and at the end of his way and his wits. Suddenly up came Gollum and whispered and hissed:

"Bless us and splash us, my preciousssss! I guess it's a choice feast; at least a tasty morsel it'd make us, gollum!" And when he said *gollum* he made a horrible swallowing noise in his throat. That is how he got his name, though he always called himself "my precious."

The hobbit jumped nearly out of his skin when the hiss came in his ears, and he suddenly saw the pale eyes sticking out at him.

"Who are you?" he said, thrusting his dagger in front of him.

"What iss he, my preciouss?" whispered Gollum (who always spoke to himself through never having anyone else to speak to). This is what he had come to find out, for he was not really very hungry at the moment, only curious; otherwise he would have grabbed first and whispered afterwards.

"I am Mr. Bilbo Baggins, I have lost the dwarfs and I have lost the wizard, and I don't know where I am; and I don't want to know, if only I can get away."

"What's he got in his handses?" said Gollum, looking at the sword, which he did not quite like.

"A sword, a blade which came out of Gondolin!"

"Sssss," said Gollum, and became quite polite. "Praps ye sits here and chats with it a bitsy, my preciousss. It like riddles, praps it does, does it?" He was anxious to appear friendly, at any rate for the moment, and until he found out more about the sword and the hobbit, whether he was quite alone really, whether he was good to eat, and whether Gollum was really hungry. Riddles were all he could think of. Asking them, and sometimes guessing them, had been the only game he had ever played with other funny creatures sitting in their holes in the long, long ago, before he lost all his friends and was driven away, alone, and crept down, down, into the dark under the mountains.

"Very well," said Bilbo, who was anxious to agree, until he found out more about the creature, whether he was quite alone, whether he was fierce or hungry, and whether he was a friend of the goblins.

"You ask first," he said, because he had not had time to think of a riddle.

So Gollum hissed:

What has roots as nobody sees,
Is taller than trees,
Up, up it goes,
And yet never grows?

"Easy!" said Bilbo. "Mountain, I suppose."

"Does it guess easy? It must have a competition with us, my preciouss! If precious asks, and it doesn't answer, we eats it, my preciousss. If it asks us, and we doesn't answer then we does what it wants eh? We shows it the way out, yes!"

"All right!" said Bilbo, not daring to disagree, and nearly bursting his brain to think of riddles that could save him from being eaten.

Thirty white horses on a red hill,
First they champ,
Then they stamp,
Then they stand still.

That was all he could think of to ask—the idea of

eating was rather on his mind. It was rather an old one, too, and Gollum knew the answer as well as you do.

"Chestnuts, chestnuts," he hissed. Teeth! teeth! my preciousss; but we has only six! Then he asked his second:

Voiceless it cries,
Wingless flutters,
Toothless bites,
Mouthless mutters.

"Half a moment!" cried Bilbo, who was still thinking uncomfortably about eating. Fortunately he had once heard something rather like this before, and getting his wits back he thought of the answer. "Wind, wind of course," he said, and he was so pleased that he made up one on the spot. "This'll puzzle the nasty little underground creature," he thought:

An eye in a blue face
Saw an eye in a green face.
"That eye is like to this eye"
Said the first eye,
"But in low place,
Not in high place."

"Ss, ss, ss," said Gollum. He had been underground a long long time, and was forgetting this sort of thing. But just as Bilbo was beginning to hope that the wretch would not be able to answer, Gollum brought up memories of ages and ages and ages before, when he lived with his grandmother in a hole in a bank by a river, "Sss, sss, my preciouss," he said. "Sun on the daisies it means, it does."

But these ordinary aboveground everyday sort of riddles were tiring for him. Also they reminded him of days when he had been less lonely and sneaky and nasty, and that put him out of temper. What is more they made him hungry; so this time he tried something a bit more difficult and more unpleasant:

It cannot be seen, cannot be felt,
Cannot be heard, cannot be smelt.
It lies behind stars and under hills
And empty holes its fills
It comes first and follows after,
Ends life, kills laughter.

"Unfortunately for Gollum Bilbo had heard that sort of thing before; and the answer was all round him any way. "Dark!" he said without even scratching his head or putting on his thinking cap.

A box without hinges, key, or lid!
Yet golden treasure inside is hid,

he asked to gain time, until he could think of a really hard one. This he thought a dreadfully easy chestnut, though he had not asked it in the usual words. But it proved a nasty poser for Gollum. He hissed to himself, and still he did not answer; he whispered and spluttered.

After some while Bilbo became impatient. "Well, what is it?" he said. "The answer's not a kettle boiling over, as you seem to think from the noise you are making."

"Give us a chance; let it give us a chance, my preciouss-ss-ss."

"Well, said Bilbo, after giving him a long chance, "what about your guess?"

But suddenly Gollum remembered thieving from nests long ago, and sitting under the river bank teaching his grandmother, teaching his grandmother, to suck—"Eggses!" he hissed. "Eggses it is!" Then he asked:

Alive without breath,
As cold as death;
Never thirsty, ever drinking,
All in mail never clinking.

He also in his turn thought this was a dreadfully easy one, because he was always thinking of the answer. But he could not remember anything better at the moment, he was so flustered by the egg-question. All the same it was a poser for poor Bilbo, who never had anything to do with the water if he could help it. I imagine you know the answer, of course, or can guess it as easy as winking, since you are sitting comfortably at home and have not the danger of being eaten to disturb your thinking. Bilbo sat and cleared his throat once or twice, but no answer came.

After a while Gollum began to hiss with pleasure to himself: "Is it nice, my preciousss? Is it juicy? Is it scrumptiously crunchable? He began to peer at Bilbo out of the darkness.

"Half a moment," said the hobbit shivering. "I gave you a good long chance just now."

"It must make haste, haste!" said Gollum, beginning to climb out of his boat on to the shore to get at Bilbo. But when he put his long webby foot in the water, a fish jumped out in a fright and fell on Bilbo's toes.

"Ugh!" he said, "it is cold and clammy!"—and so he guessed. "Fish! fish!" he cried. "It is fish!"

Gollum was dreadfully disappointed; but Bilbo asked another riddle as quick as ever he could, so that Gollum had to get back into his boat and think.

No-legs lay on one-leg, two-legs sat near on
three-legs, four-legs got some.

It was not really the right time for this riddle, but Bilbo was in a hurry. Gollum might have had some trouble guessing it, if he had asked it at another time. As it was, talking of fish, "no-legs" was not so very difficult, and after that the rest was easy. "Fish on a little table, man at table sitting on a stool, the cat has the bones" that of course is the answer, and Gollum soon gave it. Then he thought the time had come to ask something hard and horrible. This is what he said:

This thing all things devours:
Birds, beasts, trees, flowers
Gnaws iron, bites steel;
Grinds hard stones to meal;
Slays king, ruins town,
And beats high mountain down.

Poor Bilbo sat in the dark thinking of all the horrible names of all the giants and ogres he had ever heard told of in tales, but not one of them had done all these things. He had a feeling that the answer was quite different and that he ought to know it, but he could not think of it. He began to get frightened, and that is bad for thinking. Gollum began to get out of his boat. He flapped into the water and paddled to the bank; Bilbo could see his eyes coming towards him. His tongue seemed to stick in his mouth; he wanted to shout out: "Give me more time! Give me more time!" But all that came out with a sudden squeal was:

"Time! Time!"

Bilbo was saved by pure luck. For that of course was the answer.

Gollum was disappointed once more; and now he was getting angry, and also tired of the game. It had made him very hungry indeed. This time he did not go back to the boat. He sat down in the dark by Bilbo. That made the hobbit most dreadfully uncomfortable and scattered his wits.

"It's got to ask uss a question, my preciouss, yes, yess, yesss. Just one more question to guess, yes, yess" said Gollum.

But Bilbo simply could not think of any question with that nasty wet cold thing sitting next to him, and pawing and poking him. He scratched himself, he pinched himself; still he could not think of anything.

"Ask us! Ask us!" said Gollum.

Bilbo pinched himself and slapped himself; he gripped on his little sword; he even felt in his pocket with his other hand. There he found the ring he had picked up in the passage and forgotten about.

"What have I got in my pocket?" he said aloud. He was talking to himself, but Gollum thought it was a riddle, and he was frightfully upset.

"Not fair! Not fair!" he hissed. "It isn't fair,

my precious, is it, to ask us what it's got in its nassty little pocketses?"

Bilbo seeing what had happened and having nothing better to ask stuck to his question, "What have I got in my pocket?" he said louder.

"S-s-s-s-s," hissed Gollum. "It must give us three guesseses, my preciouss, three guesseses."

"Very well! Guess away!" said Bilbo.

"Handses!" said Gollum.

"Wrong," said Bilbo, who had luckily just taken his hand out again. "Guess again!"

"S-s-s-s-s," said Gollum more upset than ever. He thought of all the things he kept in his own pockets: fishbones, goblins' teeth, wet shells, a bit of bat-wing, a sharp stone to sharpen his fangs on, and other nasty things. He tried to think what other people kept in their pockets.

"Knife!" he said at last.

"Wrong!" said Bilbo, who had lost his some time ago. "Last guess!"

Now Gollum was in a much worse state than when Bilbo had asked him the egg-question. He hissed and spluttered and rocked himself backwards and forwards, and slapped his feet on the floor, and wriggled and squirmed; but still he did not dare to waste his last guess.

"Come on!" said Bilbo. "I am waiting!" He tried to sound bold and cheerful, but he did not feel at all sure how the game was going to end, whether Gollum guessed right or not.

"Time's up!" he said.

"String, or nothing!" shrieked Gollum, which was not quite fair—working in two guesses at once.

"Both wrong," cried Bilbo very much relieved; and he jumped at once to his feet, put his back to the nearest wall, and held out his little sword. He knew, of course, that the riddle-game was sacred and of immense antiquity, and even wicked creatures were afraid to cheat when they played at it. But he felt he could not trust this slimy thing to keep any promise at a pinch. Any excuse would do for him to slide out of it. And after all that last question had not been a genuine riddle according to the ancient laws.

CONVERSATIONS

What's being said here?

Picture Talk

What if our voices made images instead of sounds?
Would they be flat or three-dimensional? How long would the images last in the air?
Would picture talk be the same in every country?
Would "learning to talk" be easier or more difficult?

T.FOSTER

But what if pictures talked?

Find a picture to have a conversation with. What will you talk about?

Louis Goes to School

by E.B. White

Next morning, Sam took Louis to school with him. Sam rode his pony, and Louis flew along. At the schoolhouse, the other children were amazed to see this great bird, with his long neck, bright eyes, and big feet. Sam introduced him to the teacher of the first grade, Mrs. Hammerbotham, who was short and fat. Sam explained that Louis wanted to read and write because he was unable to make any sound with his throat.

Mrs. Hammerbotham stared at Louis. Then she shook her head. "No birds!" she said. "I've got enough trouble."

Sam looked disappointed.

"Please, Mrs. Hammerbotham," he said. "Please let him stand in your class and learn to read and write."

"Why does a bird need to read and write?" replied the teacher. "Only *people* need to communicate with one another."

"That's not quite true, Mrs. Hammerbotham,"

said Sam, "if you'll excuse me for saying so. I have watched birds and animals a great deal. All birds and animals talk to one another—they really have to, in order to get along. Mothers have to talk to their young. Males have to talk to females, particularly in the spring of the year when they are in love."

"In *love?"* said Mrs. Hammerbotham, who seemed to perk up at this suggestion. "What do *you* know about love?"

Sam blushed.

"What kind of a bird *is* he?" she asked.

"He's a young Trumpeter Swan," said Sam. "Right now he's sort of a dirty gray color, but in another year he'll be the most beautiful thing you ever saw—pure white, with black bill and black feet. He was hatched last spring in Canada and now lives in the Red Rock Lakes, but he can't say ko-hoh the way the other swans can, and this puts him at a terrible disadvantage."

"Why?" asked the teacher.

"Because it does," said Sam. "If *you* wanted to say ko-hoh and couldn't make a single solitary sound, wouldn't *you* feel worried?"

"I don't *want* to say ko-hoh," replied the teacher. "I don't even know what it means. Anyway, this is all just foolishness, Sam. What makes you think a bird can learn to read and write? It's impossible."

"Give him a chance!" pleaded Sam. "He is well behaved, and he's bright, and he's got this very serious speech defect."

"What's his name?"

"I don't know," replied Sam.

"Well," said Mrs. Hammerbotham, "if he's coming into my class, he's got to have a name. Maybe we can find out what it is." She looked at the bird. "Is your name Joe?"

Louis shook his head.

"Jonathan?"

Louis shook his head.

"Donald?"

Louis shook his head again.

"Is your name Louis?" asked Mrs. Hammerbotham. Louis nodded his head very hard and jumped up and down and flapped his wings.

"Great Caesar's ghost!" cried the teacher. "Look at those wings! Well, his name is Louis—that's for sure. All right, Louis, you may join the class. Stand right here by the blackboard. And don't mess up the room, either! If you need to go outdoors for any reason, raise one wing."

Louis nodded. The first-graders cheered. They liked the looks of the new pupil and were eager to see what he could do.

"Quiet, children!" said Mrs. Hammerbotham sternly. "We'll start with the letter *A*."

She picked up a piece of chalk and made a big **A** on the blackboard. "Now *you* try it, Louis!"

Louis grabbed a piece of chalk in his bill and drew a perfect **A** right under the one the teacher had drawn.

"You see?" said Sam. "He's an unusual bird."

"Well," said Mrs. Hammerbotham, "*A* is easy. I'll give him something harder." She wrote **CAT** on the board. "Let's see you write *cat,* Louis!"

Louis wrote *cat.*

"Well *cat* is easy, too," muttered the teacher. "*Cat* is easy because it is short. Can anyone think of a word that is longer than *cat?*"

"Catastrophe," said Charlie Nelson, who sat in the first row.

"Good!" said Mrs. Hammerbotham. "That's a good hard word. But does anyone know what it means? What *is* a catastrophe?"

"An earthquake," said one of the girls.

"Correct!" replied the teacher. "What else?"

"War is a catastrophe," said Charlie Nelson.

"Correct!" replied Mrs. Hammerbotham. "What else is?"

A very small, redheaded girl named Jennie raised her hand.

"Yes, Jennie? What is a catastrophe?"

In a very small, high voice, Jennie said, "When you get ready to go on a picnic with your father and mother and you make peanut-butter sandwiches and jelly rolls and put them in a thermos box with bananas and an apple and some raisin cookies and paper napkins and some bottles of pop and a few hard-boiled eggs and then you put the thermos box in your car and just as you are starting out it starts to *rain* and your parents say there is no point in having a picnic in the rain, that's a catastrophe."

"Very good, Jennie," said Mrs. Hammerbotham. "It isn't as bad as an earthquake, and it isn't as bad as war. But when a picnic gets called on account of rain, it *is* a catastrophe for a child, I guess. Anyway, *catastrophe* is a good word. No bird can write *that* word, I'll bet. If I can teach a bird to write *catastrophe,* it'll be big news all over the Sweet Grass country. I'll get my picture in *Life* magazine. I'll be famous."

Thinking of all these things, she stepped to the blackboard and wrote CATASTROPHE.

"O.K., Louis, let's see you write *that!"*

Louis picked up a fresh piece of chalk in his bill. He was scared. He took a good look at the word. "A long word," he thought, "is really no harder than a short one. I'll just copy one letter at a time, and pretty soon it will be finished. Besides, my life is a catastrophe. It's a catastrophe to be without a voice." Then he began writing CATASTROPHE, he wrote, making each letter very neatly. When he got to the last letter, the pupils clapped and stamped their feet and banged on their desks, and one boy quickly made a paper airplane and zoomed it into the air. Mrs. Hammerbotham rapped for order.

"Very good, Louis," she said. "Sam, it's time you went to your own classroom—you shouldn't be in my room. Go and join the fifth grade. I'll take care of your friend the swan."

Spring followed winter; summer followed spring. A year went by, and it was springtime again. Still no sign of Louis. Then one morning when Louis's grown-up brothers were playing a game of water polo, one of them looked up and saw a swan approaching in the sky.

"Ko-hoh!" cried the cygnet. He rushed to his father and mother. "Look! Look! Look!"

All the waterfowl on the lake turned and gazed up at the approaching swan. The swan circled in the sky.

"It's Louis!" said the cob. "But what is that peculiar little object hanging around his neck by a string? What is that?"

"Wait and see," said his wife. "Maybe it's a gift."

Louis looked down from the sky and spotted what looked like his family. When he was sure, he glided down and skidded to a stop. His mother rushed up and embraced him. His father arched his neck gracefully and raised his wings in greeting. Everyone shouted "Ko-hoh!" and "Welcome back, Louis!" His family was overjoyed. He had been gone for a year and a half—almost eighteen months. He looked older and handsomer. His feathers were pure white now, instead of a dirty gray. Hanging by a cord around his neck was a small slate. Attached to the slate by a piece of string was a white chalk pencil.

When the family greetings were over, Louis seized the chalk in his bill and wrote "Hi, there!" on the slate. He held the slate out eagerly for all to see.

The cob stared at it. The mother swan stared at it. The cygnets stared at it. They just stared and stared. Words on a slate meant nothing to them. They couldn't read. None of the members of his family had ever seen a slate before, or a piece of chalk. Louis's attempt to greet his family was a failure. He felt as though he had wasted a year and a half by going to school and

learning to write. He felt keenly disappointed. And, of course, he was unable to speak. The words on the slate were all he could offer by way of greeting.

Finally his father, the cob, spoke up.

"Louis, my son," he began in his deep, resonant voice, "this is the day we have long awaited—the day of your return to our sanctuary in the Red Rock Lakes. No one can imagine the extent of our joy or the depth of our emotion at seeing you again, you who have been absent from our midst for so long, in lands we know not of, in pursuits we can only guess at. How good it is to see your countenance again! We hope you have enjoyed good health during your long absence, in lands we know not of, in pursuits we can only guess at—"

"You've said that once already," said his wife. "You're repeating yourself. Louis must be tired after his trip, no matter where he's been or what he's been up to."

"Very true," said the cob. "But I must prolong my welcoming remarks a bit longer, for my curiosity is aroused by that odd little object Louis is wearing around his neck and by the strange symbols he has placed upon it by rubbing that white thing up and down and leaving those strange white tracings."

"Well," said Louis's mother, "we're *all* interested in it, naturally. But Louis can't explain it because he is defective and can't talk. So we'll just have to forget our curiosity for the moment and let Louis take a bath and have dinner."

Everyone agreed this was a good idea.

Louis swam to the shore, placed his slate and his chalk pencil under a bush, and took a bath. When he was through, he dipped the end of one wing in the water and sorrowfully rubbed out the words "Hi, there!" Then he hung the slate around his neck again.

Messages are where you find them

How would you react if you found this treasure map crumpled in a wastepaper basket? framed and hanging in someone's living room? displayed in a museum? reproduced in a history textbook? published in a newspaper?

Is the message always the same?

But what if you had found the map somewhere in this shop?

ASSEM TERCES

Sometimes
holes can be cut in card
to make a stencil. When a message has to be sent secretly, it
can be written through the holes onto
paper. So that the secret message is
hidden, another message has to be written around it. With care the secret
words fit in so well that only a
friend who has a copy of the
stencil can read the
message.

Sometimes
a mes-
sage
can be
hidden
With
in
a
message

THISMESSAGE
ISHARDTOUN
DERSTANDON
CETHEPAPER
ISUNROLLED

SEGASSEM

TERCES

cnorat ioe
ayuedhsn?

11 13-24-35-23-15-42

52-34-42-25-43 31-24-25-15 44-23-24-43

	1	2	3	4	5
1	A	B	C	D	E
2	F	G	H	I J	K
3	L	M	N	O	P
4	Q	R	S	T	U
5	V	W	X	Y	Z

so met I me sthem ess age I shid den thi sway

terces segassem

try to make up a new code or cipher

h w i h a r t e m s a e e a r e s c e l ? a y u e t i i e i a t r ?
o m g t w i t n e s g b c r i d e r t y c n o s t h s d a n s o y

13-11-33 54-34-45 43-15-33-14
11-33 24-33-51-24-43-24-12-31 15
52-42-24-44-44-15-33
32-15-43-43-11-22-15 44-34 11
21-42-24-15-33-14

make up a story in which
there is a password, a secret
signal and a ciphered
message.

ma keup astor yin w hic hac ode
dmes sageis anim porta ntc lue

metro weather

tomorrow fair
next day fair
weekend fair

Monday—Friday 48 pages

Established 1890 Circulation 482,000

School children conduct newspaper survey

Special to The Daily
by Sally Blake
Across the country today thousands of children began a survey of newspapers. A special study of headlines, lead stories and layout is expected to result in the production of student-made versions of daily papers. Some newsmen, informed of the student activity, were frankly skeptical. "Frankly," said Ron McClive of *The Daily*, "I'm skeptical. I don't think a bunch of school kids can do a newsman's job. It stands to reason. They're only kids." Other reporters were delighted by the interest children were showing. "There is plenty of newsworthy activity in the average school," said Sara Wilkins, Education Correspondent at *The Daily*. "They'll never run short of copy. Good luck to them."

Children very serious, say School Principals

Atlanta (AP)

School Principals contacted by reporters from *The Daily* unanimously agreed that their students were working hard on the newspaper survey. School Principal Leigh Jones said the children at her school were "very serious" about the project. She said they were interviewing parents, members of staff and other adults to find out how many people read newspapers regularly. "Dozens of youngsters have asked me which section of my paper I read first. I only hope they're interviewing other people as well." Mrs. Jones laughingly explained that she had finally typed a notice for the door of her office. "Now I don't have to be interviewed again. The children can get the information from the notice." Mrs. Jones said.

This scene in a Grade Five classroom was typical of many other classrooms today. Snap Gordon (photo)

What's inside?

Size of headlines and content of the news reports on pages two and three were to be examined today by children taking part in the newspaper survey. Some children, pretending to be reporters, were asked to select a second page story to rewrite as a front page headline. "I'm interested in finding out which stories go where," a schoolboy reporter was heard to say.

Where does all the news come from, children ask

Today, children throughout the city were trying to discover the meaning of the initials AP, CP, UPI, and others that sometimes appear at the beginning of news reports. Some children were investigating the significance of Reuter, New York Times Service, and other information found below the headline. Children who visited the Press Room of *The Daily* yesterday were shown how news comes in on teletype.

Crosswords make for cross words

Children complained today about how hard it was to make up good crossword puzzles.

Classified ads search

Teams of school children began an investigation of the classified advertisements that appear daily in the newspapers.

Kids make great copy
Columnists support survey
"Kids are great for human-interest stories," Bill Ease, The Daily's popular columnist said today. Mr. Ease addressed a gathering of his fellow journalists at a meeting held to demonstrate support for the recent outbreak of children-led newspaper surveys across the country. "Whenever I'm stuck for a story, I always write about something a kid has said or done. My readers love it."
Letters to the editor
Sir:
Three cheers for the younger generation. Recently, I was delighted to hear of a group of school children conducting a survey on community reading interests. They are not only finding out important information, they are developing research skills that will stand them in good stead in later life. I wish my schooldays had been as interesting.
I. Thompson, Scottsville.
Sir:
I am appalled at the time-wasting going on in the schools. The latest gimmick in my district is to allow children out of school and into the community to conduct so-called "research." In my day we stayed in the classroom to learn. Either bring down school taxes or get the kids back to work.
Janice George, Livonia.
Children chart sports coverage
"Sport is big news," said school children who had recently completed a newspaper survey. The children displayed charts to show the number of sports reported daily and those which received the most space. The charts also showed when sports news had made the front page.
One group of children had concentrated on sports photography. They planned to show in a display

Laissez le volant et venez vivre avec nous, de temps en temps: c'est si reposant.

Nos trains sont beaucoup plus qu'un moyen de transport agréable, sûr et confortable . . . c'est un mode de vie que vous découvrirez à bord.

La plupart de nos trains vous offrent divers services de repas et de boissons, et un vaste choix de voitures-lits.

Grâce aux tarifs Rouge, Blanc, Bleu, il est facile de choisir la date qui convient le mieux à votre budget. Et les billets Famille, Jeunesse, Sagesse et Groupe permettent des économies supplémentaires.

拒參共同市場

奥斯陸路透電：據昨日宣佈兩日全民投票之大致結果，挪威之漁民、農民及左派份子等，均拒絕挪威參加歐洲經濟社會。

■投票顯示選民百分之五十二點五反對參加共同市場，而百分之四十七點五則贊成。

迄晨一時四十五分，統計票數已達百分之九十六，總理布列特利即在電視上向全國廣播稱：「數字已表示挪威不能成爲市場會員，而政府必辭職；現則需由該等解決此困難之人，爲吾人解決此一困難局面矣。」

今年爲安省博物館六十週年紀念，博物館舉行一展覽。昨日開「中國古墓園置有中國色彩甚多。

Foreign language papers pour into classrooms

Wichita (UPI)

Newspapers in many different languages were taken to classrooms today. Papers in Chinese, Czechoslovakian, Dutch, Estonian, Finnish, French, German, Greek, Hebrew, Hungarian, Italian, Japanese, Korean, Latvian, Lithuanian, Polish, Portuguese, Russian, Spanish, Ukrainian and Yugoslavian were brought to school by hundreds of children. Newspapers from twenty English-speaking countries were also produced. Children who had examined some of these papers were surprised to find them similar in appearance to the ones they read at home. "I could tell right away they were newspapers," said Jill Tew, a Grade Five student, "even though I couldn't understand a word."

NÉGYEZER ÉVES CSODÁLATOS SEBÉSZET

Az ókori sebészet, mint az antropológiai vizsgálatokból kiderült, olyan magas fokon állt, mint a modern sebészet: még a sérült koponyákat is sikeresen operálták.

A legutóbb az Arméniában folytatott ásatások 3,500 éves leleteket hoztak felszínre. A Yerevani Orvosi Egyetem professzora — aki mellesleg antropológus is — érdekes megállapításokkal lepte meg a világot. A Yerevan melletti tófenék ásatásai közben a régészek többek között emberi koponyákra bukkantak, amelyeken a professzor szerint valamikor a legkényesebb fejműtétet hajtották végre. Mint a koponyák bizonyítják — kitűnő sebészeik voltak.

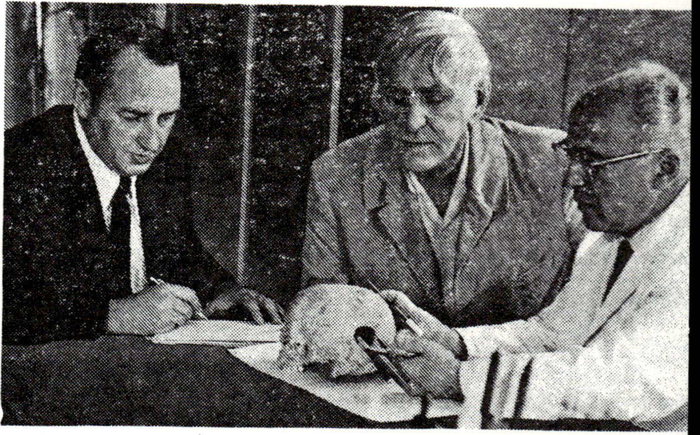

Prof. Jagharian mutatja a koponyát, amelyet 3500 évvel ezelőtt t be egy sebész

OVA ESCOLA DE PORTUGUÊS EM PLENO FUNCIONAMENTO

EM TORONTO

forme "Novo Mundo" havia noticiado na edição de 30 de Agosto fin
s uma Escola de Português em Toronto, "The Portuguese Community
aboração com as Igrejas Portuguesas de Santa Maria, Santa Inês e Santa H
os párocos, os Revs. Alberto Cunha, Antero de Melo e Alexandre Neves, re
ente, têm dado o melhor apoio e colaboração. A gravura acima mostra o mo
nício das aulas na "Santa Verónica Catholic School", com a presença dos
s, pais e alunos e ainda do Rev. Alexandre Neves, que proferiu algumas p
oas-vindas, de incitamento às crianças pelo estudo da língua portuguesa e
mento aos pais pelo entusiasmo e compreensão com que têm colaborado ne
el iniciativa.

La sicurezza dei vostri piedi dipende dalla vostra assennatezza

Pensateci.
Quando giocate a tennis calzate scarpe da tennis. Quando camminate calzate buone scarpe da passeggio e quando lavorate calzate apposite calzature per comodità e per protezione.

Osservate le vostre scarpe. Assicuratevi che i tacchi non siano consumati. Cambiate le stringhe se sono consumate. Assicuratevi che le suole siano in buone condizioni. Calzate scarpe adeguate al vostro lavoro: cio' vi darà sicurezza.

L'autodifesa dà buoni risultati.

Η ΑΚΕΡΑΙΟΤΗΣ ΤΩΝ ΠΟΔΙΩΝ ΣΑΣ ΕΞΑΡΤΑΤΑΙ ΑΠΟ ΤΗ ΦΡΟΝΗΣΗ ΣΑΣ.

Γιά σκεφθῆτε το.
Ὅταν παίζετε τέννις φορᾶτε παπούτσια τοῦ τέννις, ὅταν περπατᾶτε, φορᾶτε καλά παπούτσια πεζοπορίας. Καί ὅταν ἐργάζεσθε φορᾶτε κατάλληλα παπούτσια γιά ἄνεση ΚΑΙ ἀσφάλεια.

Εξετᾶστε τά παπούτσια σας. Μήν τά ἀφήνετε νά φθείρονται πολύ στά τακούνια. Ἀλλάξτε τά χαλασμένα κορδόνια. Καί προσέχετε νά εἶναι οἱ σόλες σέ καλή κατάσταση.
Τό σίγουρο περπάτημα ἀρχίζει μέ τά κατάλληλα παπούτσια.

Ο ΒΕΒΑΙΟΣ ΤΡΟΠΟΣ ΑΣΦΑΛΕΙΑΣ ΕΙΝΑΙ Η ΑΥΤΟ-ΑΜΥΝΑ.

Die Sicherheit Ihrer Füsse hängt von Ihrem Denken ab.

Denken Sie darüber nach.
Wenn Sie Tennis spielen, dann tragen Sie Tennisschuhe. Wenn Sie wandern, tragen Sie gute Laufschuhe. Und wenn Sie arbeiten, tragen Sie geeignete Arbeitsschuhe für Ihre Bequemlichkeit und zu Ihrem Schutz.

Sehen Sie sich einmal Ihre Schuhe genau an. Sorgen Sie dafür, daß sie nicht am Absatz abgetragen sind. Wechseln Sie ausgefranste Schuhsenkel aus und prüfen Sie die Sohlen, damit sie in gutem Zustand sind. Sichere Fußarbeit beginnt mit richtigem Schuhwerk.

DER BESTE WEG ZU IHRER SICHERHEIT IST SELBSTVERTEIDIGUNG.

Kids create comic strips

Children were very excited last week when Hatch McGuire, the cartoonist, visited schools in the area. With a few strokes of his pencil, Mr. McGuire showed the children how he brings his talking animals to life. The children quickly supplied copy for the speech balloons he drew and in no time they had created a comic strip. The children asked Mr. McGuire if he thought comic strips were always funny. "A better question to ask would be 'Are comics only funny?'" was Mr. McGuire's reply. He suggested that the children conduct a survey to find out for themselves.

What are comics about? children ask

Children throughout the country began work on finding out what comics are about. Already they have found that families are regularly featured. Some children plan to look at old newspapers to see if the subject-matter in comics has changed much over the years. Others will search foreign language papers for comic strips. "We want to find out if we can tell what they are about. Maybe some well known comic strips appear in several languages," a young researcher told our reporter.

Do cartoonists like kids?

"Are we like the kids in the comics or are they like us? That's what we want to find out," said Judy Walsh, one of the children investigating the question. The children hope to find out what cartoonists are saying—indirectly—about children. "There are clues in the way kids are drawn—their faces, clothes, the way they stand," Judy told our reporter. She went on to say that her class plans to make a collection called "Kids in Comics."

Who reads what?

"Who reads the comics?" is the first question posed by children conducting a survey of comic strip readership in their community. The children hope to find out which age groups like comics, and which comics are the most popular at different age groups.

MAKE
A CLASSROOM
NEWSPAPER
ART EDITOR
EDITOR
COPY WRITER

Pssst. Have you ever thought that mis-
typed words might be messages from another
I misstype words all the time xx ams and
what"s more I likethe look of THEM tyhem
OLIVER
STANDARD

Hello there!
You won't believe this but I'm a talking
typewriter (Actually a type-talking
typewriter) and I've got plenty to say!
The Empire
EDITOR 2
Type-taLk
tYpE-TalK
TYpe-tALk
tyPe-TalK

THE DAY
THE WORDS
BEGAN
TO FADE

THE ENTIRE WORLD DEPENDS ON MEDIA MARVEL TO KEEP THE BILLIONS OF RADIO CIRCUITS, TELEPHONE CABLES, TELEGRAPH WIRES, TELEVISION WAVES, RADAR NETWORKS, COMPUTERS, AND OTHER TECHNOLOGICAL WONDERS IN PERFECT RUNNING ORDER
MEDIA MARVEL
COMIC BOOK
DAMAGED COPY

MOST SUPERHEROES LIKE TO KEEP THEIR IDENTITY SECRET. MEDIA MARVEL WAS NO EXCEPTION
MM
MM
MM
HO HUM ··· I WONDER WHAT SUPER ADVENTURE I'LL HAVE TONIGHT
MEDIOCRE
THERE GOES MY NONSTOP ELECTRONIC WARNING SYSTEM. THERE MUST BE A MEDIA BREAKDOWN SOMEWHERE
BLEEP BLEEP— BLEEP BLEEP
BLEEP BLEEP— BLEEP BLEEP
I'LL TUNE IN MY DYNAMIC AUTOMATIC RADAR TRACKER AND FIND OUT WHERE THE TROUBLE IS.

NUMBER PLEASE? CAN I HELP YOU?

DYNAMIC AUTOMATIC WHAT?

I'M SORRY, SIR. I DO NOT HAVE A NUMBER FOR THAT PARTY

THE SIGNALS ARE GETTING STRONGER. I'LL FIND THE TROUBLE SPOT WITHOUT THE HELP OF THE DART - IT MUST HAVE BLOWN A FUSE

BLEEP BLEEP

LATER, AT PETE'S POP SHOP
PETE'S
OOPS.... THERE GOES MY HANDY ELECTRONIC LINK WITH THE POLICE
MEDIA MARVEL HERE—
WHAT'S THE TROUBLE?
POLICE H.Q. TO MEDIA MARVEL COME IN PLEASE
AD FREAKS ARE ATTACKING BILLBOARDS ALONG THE FREEWAY THEY ARE SPRAYING ADS WITH BLACK PAINT. H.Q. WANTS YOU TO LOOK INTO IT.
I'LL HIDE BEHIND HERE AND SURPRISE THE AD FREAKS
DRI
POLICE H.Q TO MEDIA MARVEL. WHAT IS THE SITUATION?
REPEAT-WHAT IS THE SITUATION?
FOR THAT
MEDIA MARVEL TO H.Q. OVER— SITUATION LOOKS BLACK!

BACK AT THE HOUSE, MEDIA MARVEL CHECKS THE STATE OF THE MEDIA WITH HIS WORLDWIDE ELECTRONIC TROUBLE SCANNER
GOODNESS GRACIOUS.... THE INTERNATIONAL UNDERWATER TELEPHONE CABLE HAS UNRAVELED
I MUST GET TO THE BOTTOM OF THIS!

MEDIOCRE HOVERS OVER THE WATER BLAZING LIGHT ON THE WAVES
HMM.... MY SUPER ELECTRONIC EXAMINER TELLS ME THIS IS THE SPOT
MM

MM

HE'S GOING TO HAVE TO PULL HIMSELF TOGETHER
MEDIA MARVEL'S A WASHOUT!
HE'LL BE OK. IT'S ALWAYS LIKE THIS WHEN HE GOES SWIMMING ALONE

HE'S GOING TO HAVE TO PULL HIMSELF TOGETHER
HE'LL BE OK. IT'S ALWAYS LIKE THIS WHEN HE GOES SWIMMING ALONE
MEDIA MARVEL'S A WASHOUT!
BLAZING
HE'S GOING TO HAVE TO PULL HIMSELF TOGETHER
MEDIA MARVEL'S A WASHOUT!

HE'S GOING TO HAVE TO
SELF TOGETHER
MEDIA MARVEL'S A WASHOUT!
HE'LL BE OK. IT'S ALWAYS LIKE THIS WHEN HE GOES SWIMMING ALONE!
COME IN MEDIA MARVEL
BLEEP BLEEP – BLEEP BLEEP
I'M RECEIVING MESSAGES ON MY NONSTOP ELECTRONIC WARNING SYSTEM, MY WORLDWIDE ELECTRONIC TROUBLE SCANNER AND MY HANDY ELECTRONIC LINK WITH THE POLICE. THANK GOODNESS MY MESSAGE-RECEIVING COMPUTER IS RECORDING THEM ALL
I'LL TUNE IN MY DYNAMIC AUTOMATIC RADAR TRACKER, LINK IT TO MY COMPUTER AND SOLVE THE PROBLEMS ONE AT A TIME

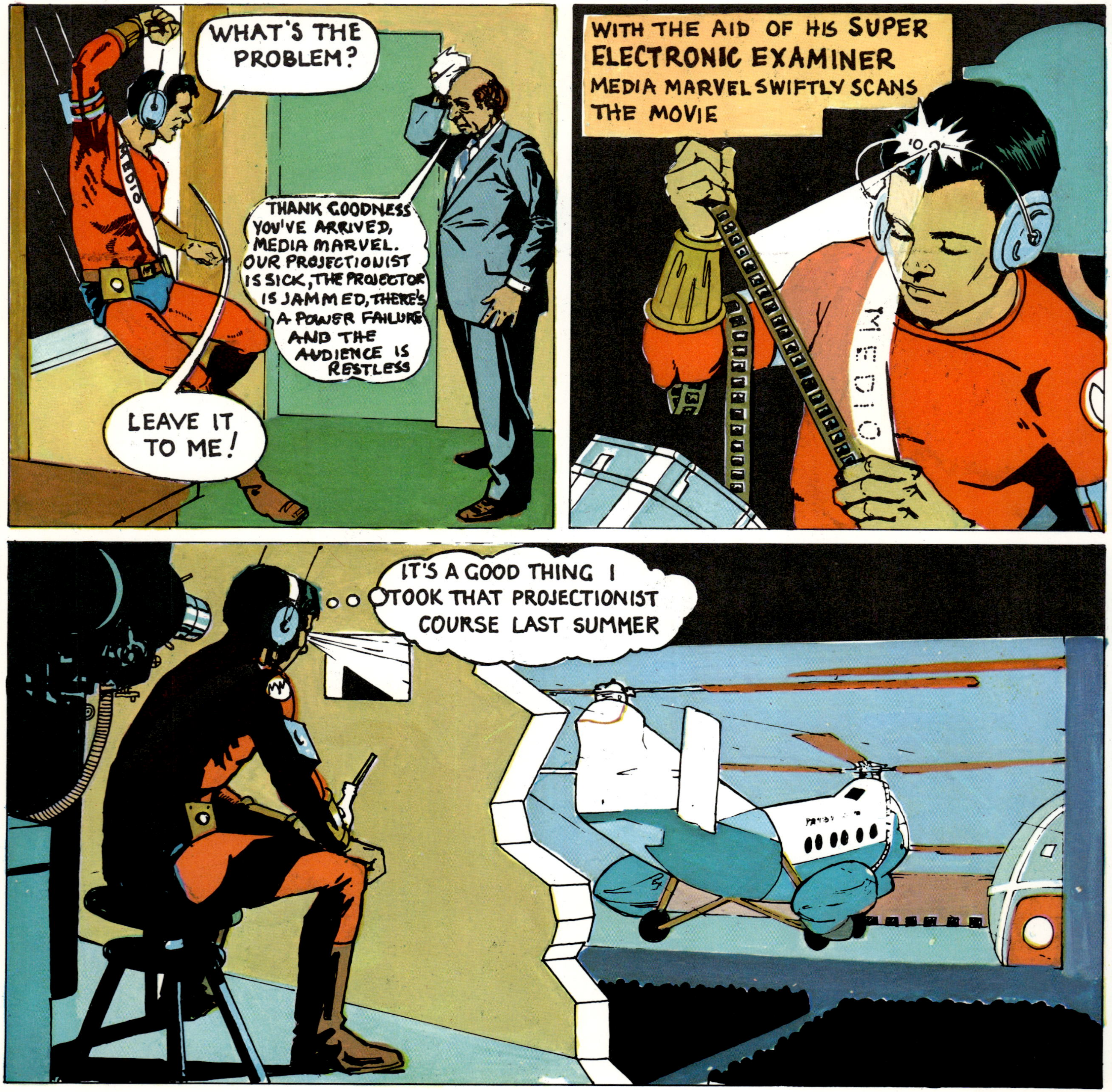

IT'S A GOOD THING I TOOK THAT PROJECTIONIST COURSE LAST SUMMER

NOW TO RESTORE THE SATELLITE TRANSMITTER
MEDIO
BLEEP BLEEP
SOMEWHERE IN SPACE....
MEDIO
H'MM .... THE NUCLEAR GENERATOR NEEDS ADJUSTING. I'LL SOON FIX THAT

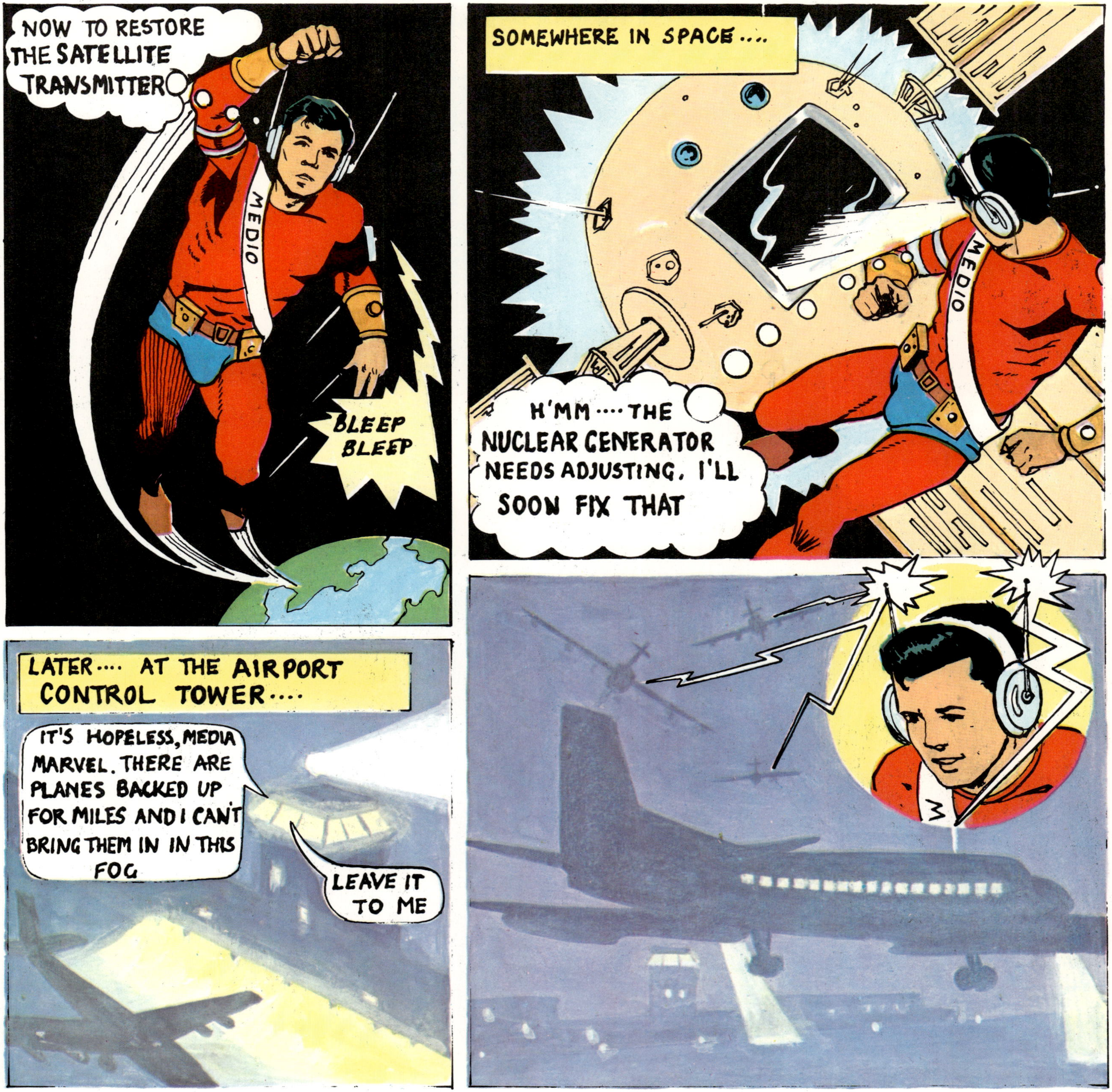

LATER.... AT THE AIRPORT CONTROL TOWER....
IT'S HOPELESS, MEDIA MARVEL. THERE ARE PLANES BACKED UP FOR MILES AND I CAN'T BRING THEM IN IN THIS FOG
LEAVE IT TO ME

OUR SOUND EQUIPMENT'S WRECKED AND WE CAN'T RECORD OUR ALBUM
MEDIO
H'MM...I THINK I HAVE THE ANSWER.... HAND ME THOSE WIRES
MEDIA MARVEL BRINGS MIGHTY POWERS OF CONCENTRATION TO THE TASK OF REPRODUCING SOUND WAVES
MEDIO
YAWN!....THINGS WERE A BIT SLOW TONIGHT
MEDIO
I HOPE THERE'S MORE ACTION TOMORROW
NEXT ISSUE.... MEDIA MARVEL MEETS THE MEDIA EVIL WOMAN
CAN MEDIA MARVEL'S ELECTRONIC POWERS WITHSTAND THE DARK FORCES OF ANOTHER TIME?

WHAT'S A PACKAGE FOR?

DRESSING UP THE GOODS

WHY IS FOOD PACKAGED FOR SALE?

DOES COLOR MAKE A DIFFERENCE?

What do the words tell?

WHAT ARE PACKAGES MADE OF?

HOW IMPORTANT IS DESIGN?

What happens to empty packages?

Why this shape?
Why this shape?
HOW IMPORTANT IS DESIGN?
Why have brand names?
MAKE A PACKAGE SURVEY.
WHY HAVE BRAND NAMES?
why this shape?
WHAT ABOUT SIZE?

SPILLING THE BEANS

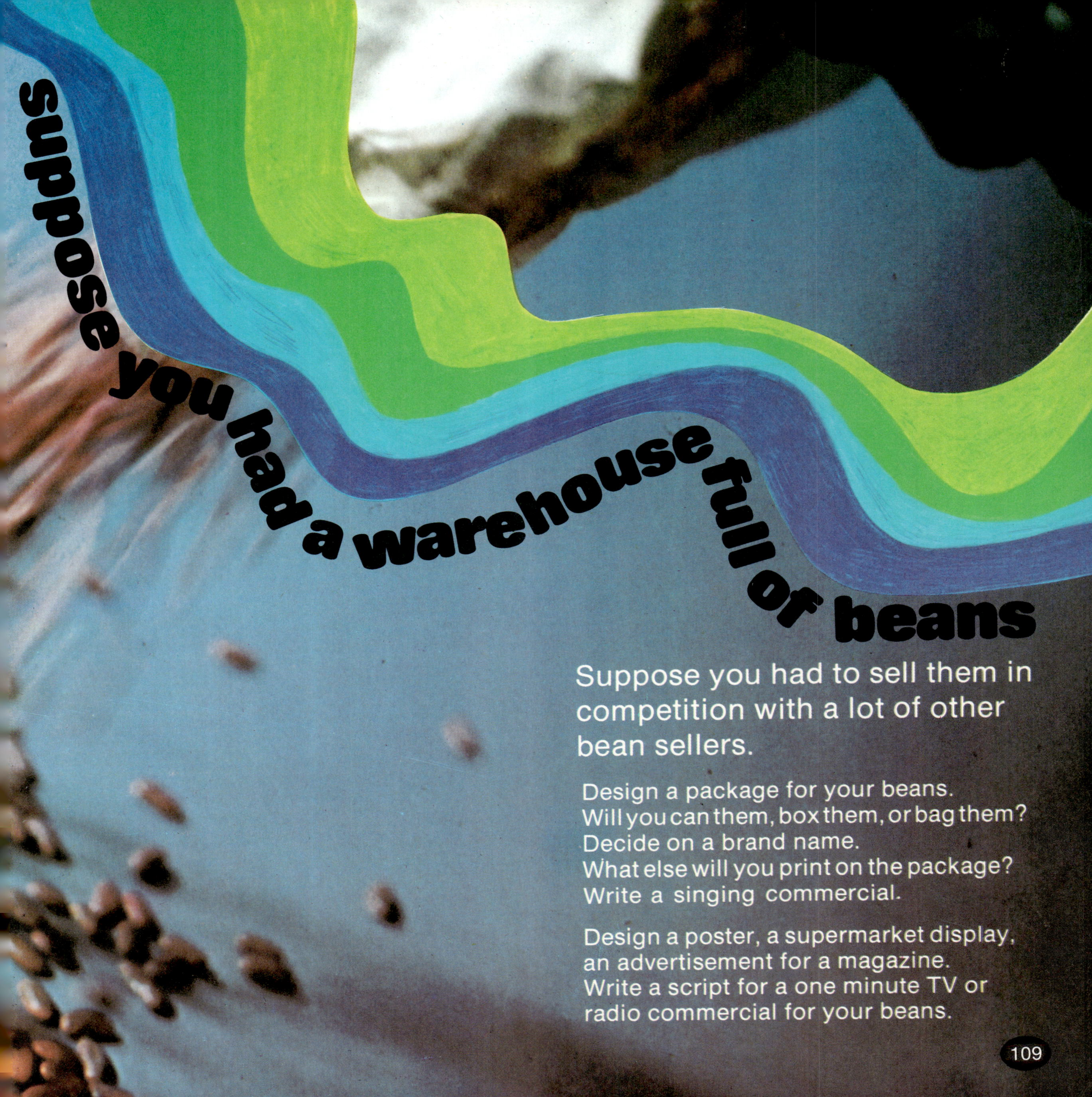

Suppose you had a warehouse full of beans

Suppose you had to sell them in competition with a lot of other bean sellers.

Design a package for your beans.
Will you can them, box them, or bag them?
Decide on a brand name.
What else will you print on the package?
Write a singing commercial.

Design a poster, a supermarket display, an advertisement for a magazine.
Write a script for a one minute TV or radio commercial for your beans.

NATIONAL NUM NUM WEEK (EXCEPT NOVA SCOTIA)
NATIONAL NUM NUM WEEK (EXCEPT NOVA SCOTIA)
NATIONAL NUM NUM WEEK (EXCEPT NOVA SCOTIA)
SPECIAL MIXED CARROTS AND SQUASH
CREAMED MENTH (CREME DE MENTHE)
WEE WHIP
WHEE!
GM ENORMOFOAM NOW WITH SESAME-LIKE SEEDS
BLUE LIQUID GRINGE
B.C. MIXED NECTARS PRUNE DATE FIG RAISIN KELP
NOW 17% MORE MONUMENTAL HIPPOWHIP INSTANT PLASTIFOAM
4
P PETITES POIS
NATIONAL TRY IT YOU LIKE IT WEEK JAN 17 - APR 2
PUDDYTAT NUM NUM
TOYOKA EGGPLANT HEARTS
SEAGIRT YOGHURT
CLOSE PINS
HARMONY GRITS
FIG FRONDS
PRESOAKED HEAD LETTUCE
RAMP SPEED 30
WHOPPING TOPPING
MOTHER COHENS WHOPPING TOPPING NU ECRU
BC PRUNE NECTAR
FINE FOR TAKING
OURS
SELF RAISING GARGANTUAN FREE FLOATING KREEMWIP INSTANT MERINGUE
CCM ROLLER BEARING
FLYER
I tried it I dint like it
GIVE UP FOR LENT
DIET FIG WIP
BARRON TORONTO STAR

Getting into TV
OFF
ON
VHF
What if you could join your favorite program? What might happen?

WHAT IF A MAGIC SWITCH BROUGHT TV CHARACTERS INTO THE ROOM?

NEW
HIGH
85
WARM
AIR
VERT
HORIZ.

ONCE UPON A TV SCREEN

IF YOU COULD PLAY A PROGRAM OVER AND OVER AGAIN - WHICH WOULD IT BE?
WHICH PROGRAMS WOULD YOU STORE ON VIDEOTAPE FOR FUTURE GENERATIONS TO VIEW?

how many ways
can you shape an idea?

shape an idea

shape an idea that can be read from different directions
shape an idea that can be read from all sides
shape an idea that moves
shape an idea that stands still but seems to move
shape an idea that changes as you move around it

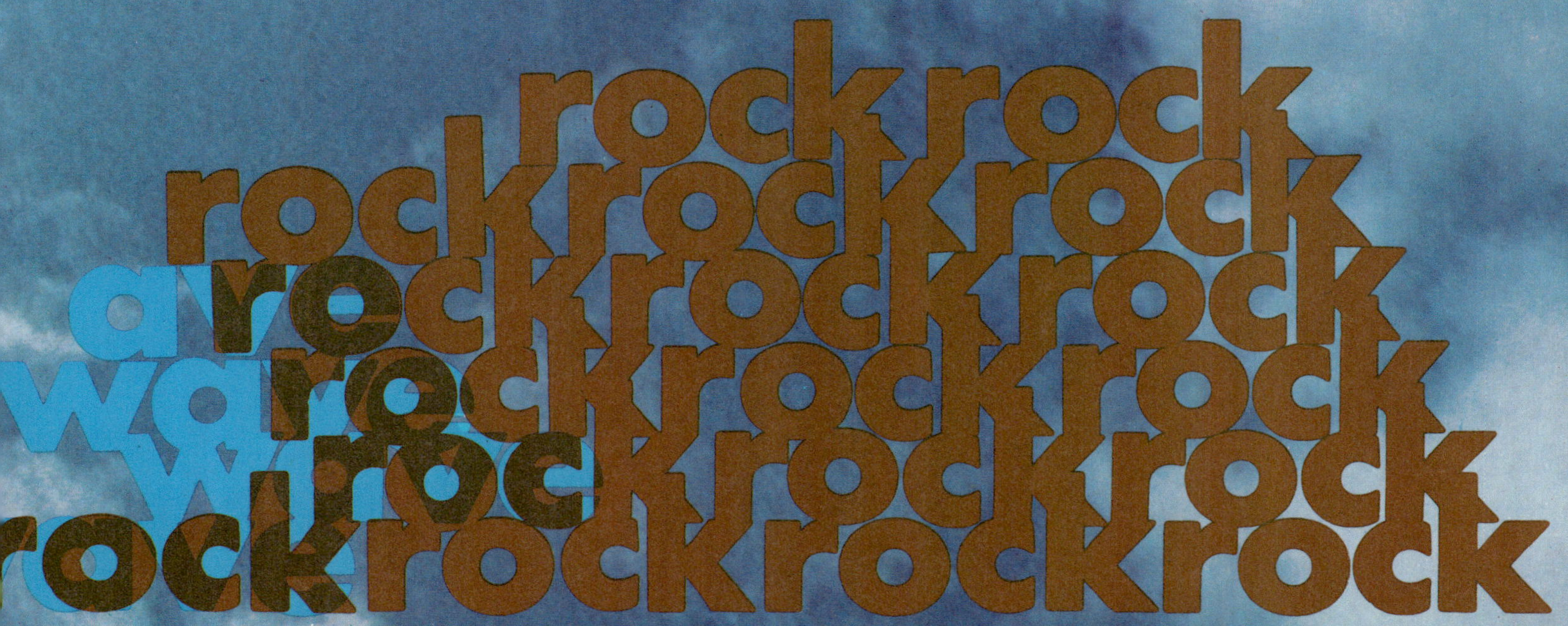

wave/rock by Ian Hamilton Finlay

SHAPE
AN
IDEA

WORDSCAPES

Water Picture

In the pond in the park
all things are doubled:
Long buildings hang and
wriggle gently. Chimneys
are bent legs bouncing
on clouds below. A flag
wags like a fishhook
down there in the sky.

The arched stone bridge
is an eye, with underlid
in the water. In its lens
dip crinkled heads with hats
that don't fall off. Dogs go by,
barking on their backs.
A baby, taken to feed the
ducks, dangles upside-down,
a pink balloon for a buoy.

Treetops deploy a haze of
cherry bloom for roots,
where birds coast belly-up
in the glass bowl of a hill;
from its bottom a bunch
of peanut-munching children
are suspended by their
sneakers, waveringly.

A swan, with twin necks
forming the figure three,
steers between two dimpled
towers doubled. Fondly
hissing, she kisses herself,
and all the scene is troubled;
water-windows splinter,
tree-limbs tangle, the bridge
folds like a fan.

May Swenson

Make pictures with words.
Write words about pictures.

Perform it: to sound effects, to music, to mime, to dance. Create lighting effects.

IT BY YOURSELF
WITH OTHERS
SHOUT IT
it
CHANT IT
whisper it
Sing it

EVERYBODY HAS A SONG TO SING
Ev'ry bo-dy has a song to sing.
Ev'ry body's song is new.
I've a special world to sing a-bout, do you? Do
you? I can sing a-bout

Sing a new song.
What will you sing about?
Will you perform alone or with a group?
Will you invite your audience to sing along with you?
Will you invent your own musical instruments, or use the ones at school and home?
How might you record your performance?

WORDSCAPES!
QUICK! WHERE'S THE CAMERA?
IF WE CAN'T DANCE IT – WE'LL PAINT IT
SAY IT WITH MIME
LET'S BRING THE TYPEWRITER TO LIFE
I'LL USE A MAGAZINE FORMAT
RED
WE'LL SHAPE OUR MESSAGES
WE'LL NEED
MOBILES
AND
SUPER MOBILES

BIG PROD

SET IT TO MUSIC
POSTERS— BANNERS— BUTTONS AND BOARDS— SANDWICH BOARDS
THIS CALLS FOR A FULL PAGE ADVERTISEMENT
WHAT ABOUT A PUPPET BALLET?
THERE'LL BE PERFORMING COMICSTRIP CHARACTERS
LET'S MAKE PUPPETS OF PEOPLE
AND PERFORMING POETS
THE MESSAGE MUST GET THROUGH
I'LL SCULPT
VIDEOTAPE?
HOW WOULD IT LOOK ON TELEVISION?
WE COULD MAKE A MUSICAL
WE'LL HAVE A POETRY AND SONG FESTIVAL

UCTIONS

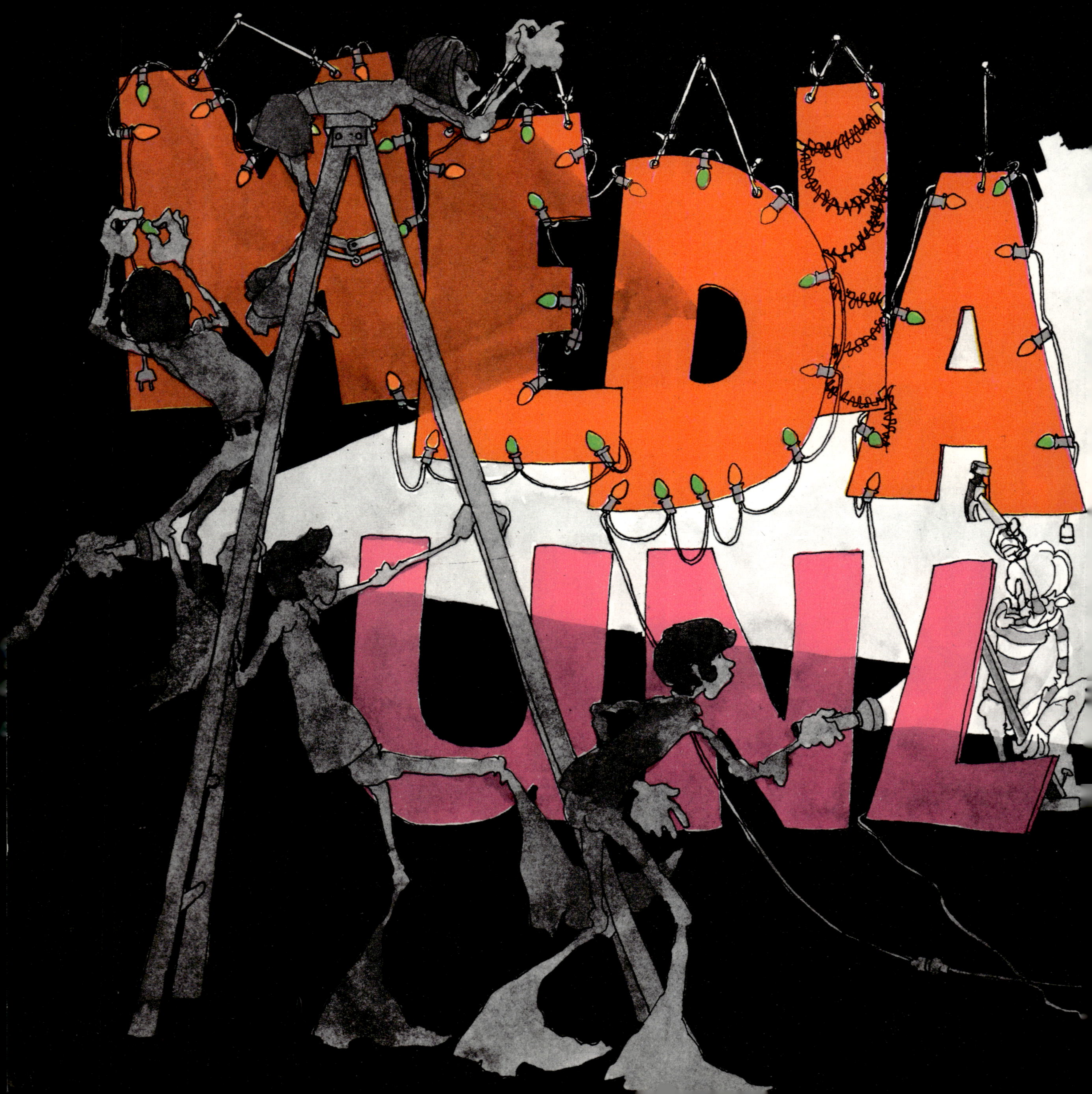
MEDIA
UNL

A BIG PRODUCTION
TV 1

Acknowledgments:

"Monkey Messages" from *The New Noah* by Gerald Durrell. Copyright 1953, 1954 by Gerald Durrell. All rights reserved. Reprinted by permission of The Viking Press, Inc. and Collins Publishers, London.

"She Can't See! She Can't Hear!" from *The Miracle Worker* by William Gibson. Reprinted by permission of Atheneum Publishers.

"When Words Began" from *The Story of My Life* by Helen Keller. Reprinted by permission of Doubleday and Company, Inc.

"Riddles in the Dark" from *The Hobbit* by J. R. R. Tolkein. Copyright © 1966 by J. R. R. Tolkein. Reprinted by permission of the publishers, Houghton Mifflin Company and George Allen and Unwin Ltd.

"Louis Goes to School" from *The Trumpet of the Swan* by E.B. White. Copyright © 1970 by E.B. White. Reprinted by permission of Harper & Row, Publishers.

Cartoon by Barron reprinted by permission of *The Toronto Star.*

"wave/rock" by Ian Hamilton Finlay reprinted by permission of the author.

"Water Picture" from *To Mix with Time* by May Swenson. Copyright © 1965 by May Swenson. Reprinted by permission of Charles Scribner's Sons.

Every effort has been made to trace the ownership of copyright material used in this book, and to make full acknowledgment for its use. The publishers will welcome any information that will allow them to correct errors or omissions in the acknowledgments.

Photo Credits:

Courtesy of American Foundation for the Blind—44
Hedy Campbell—17, 48
Ralph G. Campbell—11, 12, 15, 16, 20, 21, 23, 24-25, 26, 27, 39, 46-47, 48, 49, 59, 68-69, 72-73, 80, 81, 85, 86, 90, 91, 105, 106-107, 108-109, 110, 116-117, 120-121, 122-123
Rudi Cristl—15
Gary Fiegehen—48, 49, 118-119
Gail Johnstone—17
Information Canada, Photothèque—39
Patrick Knox—92-93, 126-127
Vladyana Krykorka—15, 40, 41
National Film Archive—30, 36, 42, 45
Frank Newberry—40, 41
Ronald Perkins—14, 18-19, 28, 120-121

Color materials from major television productions supplied through the courtesy of CTV.
Mime photographs courtesy of Paul Gallin.

Design and Illustrations:

Alan Daniel
Bob Frank
Frank Kodras
Vladyana Krykorka
Merle Smith
Marion Spanjerdt
Daniel, Knox and Frank, Inc.